Test Prep

Grade 2

Flash Kids

Spark Educational Publishing
A Division of Barnes & Noble Publishing

ISBN 1-4114-0398-3

Please submit changes or report errors to *www.sparknotes.com/errors*
For more information, please visit *www.flashkidsbooks.com*

Printed and bound in China

Spark Educational Publishing
A Division of Barnes & Noble Publishing
120 Fifth Avenue
New York, NY 10011

TABLE OF CONTENTS

FOR TEST-SMART PARENTS

As you know, standardized tests are an important part of your child's school career. These tests are created by your state's education department and set to its standards of learning for each grade level. These tests are valuable tools that measure how much your child knows in the areas of reading, writing, and math. *Test Prep: Grade 2* is designed to help your child become familiar with what tests look like. This workbook will also help your child review the basic skills taught in the second grade.

Preparation is the key to helping your child become test-smart. Practicing basic skills in a testing situation can help ensure that your child's scores will reflect his or her understanding of the material presented in school. Test-smart students:

- are comfortable in the testing environment;
- know how to approach different kinds of test questions;
- apply knowledge to a variety of test formats;
- use time wisely during tests.

ABOUT THIS WORKBOOK

Test Prep: Grade 2 is divided into two helpful sections. Practice exercises and mini-tests introduce and review basic test-taking skills. At the end of the book are longer practice tests that mirror the actual tests your child will encounter at school.

- **Units 1–7: Mini-Tests**
  Each unit focuses on a subject found on standardized tests: word study skills, reading comprehension, mathematics, listening, and language. These mini-tests help your child learn specific test strategies. Most units conclude with a unit test that covers all of the skills in the unit's lessons.

- **Units 8–13: Practice Tests**
  These longer practice tests help your child apply test-taking skills in a realistic testing environment. You and your child will work together to simulate the actual experience of taking a standardized test. By familiarizing your child with the experience, these practice tests can lessen feelings of intimidation during school tests.

USING THIS WORKBOOK WITH YOUR CHILD

You may wish to help your child read the directions, test passages, or answer choices. When your child is taking the practice tests, you might supervise the test by reading the directions and samples and briefly reviewing solution strategies.

FIND THE RIGHT QUESTION

Make sure that your child is filling in the correct answer circles when answering test questions directly in the workbook. You might begin by asking your child to point to the question number and the answer choices. Also make sure that your child darkens the circles properly.

DO NOT RUSH

Help your child relax and take time to answer each question. Some second graders hurry to respond and may not read all of the answer choices carefully. Remind your child to slow down while taking the mini-tests in the first part of this book and read every answer before choosing one.

LOOK FOR TEST TIPS

You will see helpful Test Tips throughout this workbook. Read them aloud to draw your child's attention to these useful ways to approach individual problems. The Test Tips provide hints and ideas to help your child find the best answers. They do not appear in the final practice tests, which reflect realistic testing situations.

FOUR PRINCIPLES OF TEST-TAKING

These tests help your child develop four important skills that are crucial in testing situations. Familiarize yourself with these goals in order to support your child's development of these skills.

USING TIME WISELY

All standardized tests are timed. Your child needs to understand how to manage time wisely. Review these strategies together:

- Work rapidly but comfortably.
- Do not spend too much time on any one question.
- Mark items to return to if there is enough time.
- Use any remaining time to review answers.
- Use a watch to keep track of time.

AVOIDING ERRORS

Your child can practice these strategies when choosing the correct answers on standardized tests:

- Pay careful attention to directions.
- Determine what is being asked.
- Mark answers in the appropriate place.
- Check all answers.
- Do not make stray marks on the answer sheet.

REASONING

Standardized tests require your child to think logically when answering each question. These strategies can help your child think through each question before choosing the best answer:

- Before answering a question, read the entire question or passage and all the answer choices.
- Restate questions and answer choices in your own words.
- Apply skills learned in class and practice situations.

GUESSING

Your child can learn the best thing to do when the correct answer is not clear right away. Suggest these hints as helpful solutions if a question seems difficult:

- Try to answer all of the questions within the allotted time. Do not spend too much time on a question that seems hard.
- Eliminate answers that you know are incorrect. If you cannot do this, skip the question.
- Compare the remaining answers. Restate the question, and then choose the answer that seems most correct.

With encouragement and support, your child will feel confident. Every student needs much experience with reading and exposure to a wide variety of reading material. The school curriculum is carefully designed to teach skills your child needs to become a proficient learner. Your home environment is another essential part of the education equation. Here are some ways you can help your child year-round.

CREATE A QUIET STUDY SPACE

A quiet, clean, and cheerful study space will help your child develop strong study habits. Provide a study area with an open workspace. Make sure that writing supplies like paper and pencils are nearby, as well as tools like a calculator, ruler, scissors, glue, crayons, and a dictionary. You might also create files or boxes to store your child's work. Make separate files for finished works and works in progress.

BE A HOMEWORK HELPER

Talk about homework assignments with your child. Your questions can help your child focus on what is important about the task or project. Your interest in schoolwork will encourage your child's enthusiasm and dedication. Check in while your child is working to see if you can answer any questions or help find solutions. Just letting your child know that you care can promote active learning.

MAKE READING A FAMILY HABIT

Reading every day is an activity the family can enjoy together. It will also strengthen your child's performance in school. Careful attention to the reading process helps your child achieve success when taking both language arts and math tests. Together you can read passages from schoolwork or from books your child is currently enjoying. Add reading time to your family schedule, when family members read whatever they like. When the time is up, everyone can share an interesting new fact or quotation.

PRACTICE WITH A DICTIONARY

A children's dictionary designed especially for young readers is a helpful tool for learning about words and alphabetical order. When your child does not know the meaning of a word, encourage him or her to look it up in a dictionary. Help your child discover new words. You can try this game for fun. Take turns opening the dictionary to a random page. Read a definition aloud. Can your child guess the word?

TALK ABOUT TESTS

Find out from your child's teacher when standardized tests will be given during the school year. Mark the dates on your calendar so that both you and your child know when test day approaches. Try not to schedule big activities for the night before a test.

To prepare for the yearly standardized test, score your child's work in this workbook together. Then talk about questions that were easy, hard, or tricky. Review any items your child answered incorrectly, and work together to understand why another answer is better.

A GOOD NIGHT'S SLEEP

Your child will be more relaxed and alert after a full night of sleep. Some physical exercise before dinner can relieve feelings of stress. Do not place too much emphasis on the upcoming test, but answer any questions your child may have and provide reassurance that your child is ready for the test. Reminders of what to expect may lower anxiety. Help your child choose clothing for the next day, and have it ready so there is no last-minute hunting in the morning.

FOOD FOR THOUGHT

Studies show a direct link between eating a balanced breakfast and student performance. Children who eat a good breakfast are alert in class, concentrate well, and recall information. These skills are useful at any time of the year, but are especially helpful on test day. To make sure your child eats a balanced breakfast, wake up early enough to leave plenty of time for a relaxed meal together.

SUPPORT YOUR CHILD

Remind your child that standardized tests do not measure intelligence. They measure what your child knows about some subject. Make sure that your child understands that some words or ideas on the test may be unfamiliar. Tell your child not to become frustrated or angry if a question is hard but simply try to find the answer that makes the most sense. Do not set specific goals or offer rewards for high scores. Instead, assure your child that you will be happy with a positive and wholehearted effort. Doing one's best is what really counts!

AFTER THE TEST

Be sure to talk about the test score with your child. Remind your child that no single test score gives a complete picture of how much someone knows. Help your child set goals to maintain or improve test scores in the future. Always praise your child for working hard on a test. Test scores might suggest that your child needs improvement in a specific skill or subject. Talk with your child's teacher to find ways to support your child's growth in a particular area.

Six Reading Skills

Skill 1: Determining Word Meanings

Suffixes are parts of some words. A *suffix* is at the end of a word. You can use suffixes to tell what the words mean.

Our class went on a trip to the zoo. We saw some monkeys climb into a tree. One monkey climbed <u>higher</u> than the others.

1 **In this paragraph, the word <u>higher</u> means —**

○ more than high.

○ lower.

○ almost as high.

○ on the ground.

Hint: The suffix "er" means more than.

Goldilocks walked into the three bears' home. She sat down at their table. She would not eat Papa Bear's food because it was the <u>warmest</u>.

2 **In this paragraph, the word <u>warmest</u> means —**

○ the least warm.

○ more than warm.

○ the most warm.

○ cool.

Hint: The suffix "est" means the most.

José walked up to the starting line for the foot race. He really wanted to win. José knew how important it was to run <u>quickly</u>. At the sound of the "bang" the race began.

3 **In this paragraph, the word <u>quickly</u> describes —**

○ how he will walk.

○ how he wanted to win.

○ how the race began.

○ how he will run.

Hint: When you see "ly" at the end of a word, it usually describes an action word.

GO ON ➡

Mei was getting ready for her birthday party. She invited all of her friends to come. Mei and her mother <u>baked</u> the cupcakes. They were very excited about her party.

4 **In this paragraph, the word <u>baked</u> means —**

   ○ the cupcakes were made already.

   ○ the cupcakes were not made yet.

   ○ they were making the cupcakes now.

   ○ they will not bake the cupcakes.

Hint: The suffix "ed" shows that something has already happened.

Angela's class went to the school library to take its class picture. Angela was tall, so she stood in the second row. Her friend Sulky was <u>taller</u>, so she stood in the third row.

5 **In this paragraph, the word <u>taller</u> means —**

   ○ more than tall.

   ○ the most tall.

   ○ not tall at all.

   ○ the least tall.

Hint: When you see "er" at the end of a word, what does that mean?

Kai and his mother are having fun on the playground in the park. Kai went down the slide. Then, he ran through the maze. Now he is <u>swinging</u> on the swings.

6 **In this paragraph, the word <u>swinging</u> means —**

   ○ it already took place.

   ○ it is taking place right now.

   ○ it did not take place yet.

   ○ it will never take place.

Hint: The suffix "ing" shows that something is happening now.

TEST TIP

Be sure to look for the Test Tips throughout this workbook. They will give you more test-taking strategies and specific help with certain subject areas.

GO ON ⇒

SKILL 1: DETERMINING WORD MEANINGS

Sometimes you can find out the meaning of a new word by using the words around it as clues.

Martin Luther King was a great man. He did not give up when things became <u>hard</u> for him. He did not let anyone stop him from helping others.

1   In this paragraph, the word <u>hard</u> means —

○ simple.

○ late.

○ not easy.

○ fun.

Hint: You get a clue about the word <u>hard</u> by reading sentences 2 and 3.

There are many kinds of sharks. Some are <u>huge</u>. The whale shark grows 60 feet long. That is more than the height of most houses. Only whales are larger.

2   In this paragraph, the word <u>huge</u> means —

○ big.

○ small.

○ pretty.

○ fast.

Hint: You get a clue about the word <u>huge</u> by the words "60 feet long" and by reading sentences 4 and 5.

There are many ways that fire can help us. It can keep us warm. We can cook with it. But, it can also <u>harm</u> us. It can even burn down houses.

3   In this paragraph, the word <u>harm</u> means —

○ help us.

○ warm us.

○ fool us.

○ hurt us.

Hint: You get a clue about the word <u>harm</u> by reading the last sentence.

GO ON

We have a new cat. His name is Fluffy. I want him to learn to listen to me and do what I tell him. Fluffy should learn to obey.

4 **In this paragraph, the word obey means —**

○ run away.

○ play.

○ follow directions.

○ be quiet.

Hint: You get a clue as to what the word obey means from the words "listen to me" and "do what I tell him."

Lisa loved to play baseball. She knew she could strike the ball with the bat when it was thrown to her. She decided to join the team.

5 **In this paragraph, the word strike means —**

○ to hit.

○ to miss.

○ to block.

○ to catch.

Hint: You get a clue as to what the word strike means by looking at the words "she knew she could strike the ball with the bat..."

Amy was the new girl in the class. Mira showed her where to find things around the classroom. Mira was kind to Amy.

6 **In this paragraph, the word kind means —**

○ helpful.

○ mean.

○ quiet.

○ lazy.

Hint: You get a clue as to what the word kind means by looking at what Mira did for Amy.

TEST TIP

Test these answers by replacing the word in the example. For example, look at question 6. Think of the underlined word as a blank to fill in: Mira was _____ to Amy.

Which of the four answers makes the most sense in this blank?

GO ON

SKILL 1: DETERMINING WORD MEANINGS

Special or technical words are used in science and social studies. You can use the information in the passage to tell what the words mean.

Andy dug a hole and put a plant in it. Next, he filled the hole with dirt. Last, Andy watered the plant. He made sure to soak it so that it would grow.

1   **In this paragraph, the word soak means —**

○ to dry out.

○ to cover with dirt.

○ to dig deep.

○ to make wet.

Hint: You get a clue as to what soak means by reading the sentence before the word.

Omar knew he could have a snack when he got to the end of his homework. He did his math. Then, he did his reading. Last, he ate.

2   **In this paragraph, the word end means —**

○ start.

○ finish.

○ middle.

○ test.

Hint: You get a clue as to what the word end means by reading the sentences after the word.

There are many kinds of dams. A dam can be hard to build. Some are put together with dirt while others are made from rock.

3   **In this paragraph, the word build means —**

○ to sell.

○ to climb.

○ to see.

○ to make.

Hint: You get a clue as to what build means by reading the sentence after the word.

GO ON ➡

Mandy was in a bad mood. Her mother was angry with her. Toshi called her on the telephone and told her a joke. Then Mandy started to grin.

4   In this paragraph, grin means —

○ cry.

○ see.

○ smile.

○ frown.

Hint: You get a clue about what grin means by reading the sentence before the word.

The frog leaped into the air to chase the fly. It hopped over tall grass and rocks. The frog kept leaping until it caught the fly.

5   In this paragraph, leaped means —

○ walked.

○ skipped.

○ jumped.

○ crawled.

Hint: You can get a clue about what leaped means by reading the sentences after the word.

Joy was taking a spelling test. There were two words she did not know. She wanted to quit, but she didn't. Joy kept on going.

6   In this paragraph, the word quit means —

○ scream.

○ copy.

○ stop.

○ smile.

Hint: You get a clue about what quit means by reading sentences 3 and 4.

TEST TIP

If you have trouble with one question, skip it and go back to it later. You might find it easier when you see it again.

Facts or details are important. By finding them, you will know what the passage is about.

Long ago, ships were made from logs. The center was cut out. People sat inside. They could not go very fast. These ships were also hard to make.

Things changed 5,000 years ago. They started making better ships in Egypt. These ships had sails. People could also row them. Now, they could go much faster across the water.

1   **Faster boats were first built —**

   ○ 5,000 years ago.

   ○ today.

   ○ from logs.

   ○ 500 years ago.

   Hint: Look at the second paragraph.

2   **The first ships —**

   ○ went very fast.

   ○ had sails.

   ○ could be rowed.

   ○ were hard to make.

   Hint: Read the first paragraph.

3   **The ships made in Egypt were better because —**

   ○ they were made from logs.

   ○ they were built 5,000 years ago.

   ○ they went faster.

   ○ their centers were cut out.

   Hint: Look at the last sentence.

GO ON

The first airplane flew on December 17, 1903. It was built by Wilbur and Orville Wright. They were brothers who had always dreamed of flying a plane.

Wilbur and Orville played with flying toys when they were young boys. Their mother made them play with their toys outside. They even wanted to fly the toys in the house.

As they grew up, they still wanted to fly. They worked very hard to build an airplane. One day it was ready. They tried to fly it on December 14. It did not work. Three days later, they were able to take off!

4   Wilbur and Orville Wright both wanted to —

○ stay young.

○ play with toys.

○ fly an airplane.

○ listen to their mother.

Hint: Look at the last sentence of the first paragraph.

5   Wilbur and Orville were —

○ brothers.

○ cousins.

○ friends.

○ uncles.

Hint: Look at the first paragraph.

6   Wilbur and Orville's airplane —

○ flew on December 14, 1903.

○ flew indoors.

○ was just a toy.

○ flew on December 17, 1903.

Hint: Read the first sentence.

TEST TIP

Sometimes you are allowed to write on the test pages. Before a test begins, ask your teacher if you are allowed to write on the pages. You might circle important dates or facts as you read.

GO ON

It is helpful to put events in the order in which they happened. This may help you to understand a passage.

Babe Ruth was a great baseball player. He was born on February 6, 1895. He had seven brothers and sisters. His mother became sick. Babe was sent away to school.

Babe learned to play baseball. He became a very good player. When he was 19 years old, Babe got money to play baseball.

Babe started out as a pitcher. He could throw the ball very hard. He could also hit the ball very far. Many teams wanted Babe to play for them.

In 1919, Babe started to play for the New York Yankees. He was a star player for over 15 years. In 1927 he set the home run record. This record was not broken until 1961. He was the star of the 1932 World Series. Babe Ruth was one of the best baseball players ever.

1   **Which of these happened first in the story?**

○ The 1932 World Series was played.

○ Babe was sent away to school.

○ Babe Ruth was given money to play baseball.

○ The home run record was broken.

Hint: Look at the beginning of the story.

GO ON

2 When did Babe Ruth start to play for the New York Yankees?

○ when he first learned to play baseball

○ when his mother became sick

○ in 1919

○ in 1927

Hint: Look at the last paragraph.

3 Which of these happened last?

○ Babe was a star in the World Series.

○ Babe set the home run record.

○ Many teams wanted Babe to play for them.

○ Babe's home run record was broken.

Hint: Look at the last paragraph.

TEST TIP

To answer question 3, look back at the story. Notice that the story tells the events in order, from first to last. Read the answer choices and find the one that happens <u>last</u> in the story.

GO ON ▶

Written directions tell you how to do something. Every step is important.

Did you ever make a puppet? It is a lot of fun and easy to do. There are only a few things you will need.

First, look around your house to find what you will need. Use an old sock for the body. Next, sew on buttons for the eyes. Then, glue on pieces of cloth for the mouth and ears. Last, glue yarn to the sock for hair.

1   What should you do after you find a sock?

○ glue on pieces of cloth for the mouth and ears

○ look around the house to find what you need

○ sew on buttons for the eyes

○ glue yarn to the sock for hair

Hint: Read the third sentence of the second paragraph.

Gwen needed to pack for her trip. She wrote down all the things she would need. Next, she took out her suitcase. Gwen folded her clothes on the bed. Now she was ready to pack. When she was done, she closed the suitcase. Gwen was ready for her trip!

2   To get ready for her trip, Gwen should first —

○ make a list.

○ fold her clothes.

○ close her suitcase.

○ pack her suitcase.

Hint: Read the passage to see what comes first.

GO ON

I painted my room. I wrote down the steps that I took to get the job done.

Step 1: Go to the paint store.

Step 2: Choose a color.

Step 3: Buy the paint and brushes.

Step 4: Cover things in your room. You do not want to get paint on them.

Step 5: Paint slowly. Make sure you do a careful job.

Step 6: Clean the brushes with soap and water.

Step 7: Wait for the paint to dry.

3 Which of these would you do first?

○ Clean the brushes with soap and water.

○ Buy the paint and brushes.

○ Wait for the paint to dry.

○ Cover things in your room.

Hint: Read all the steps in order.

4 When should you start to paint?

○ Step 3

○ Step 4

○ Step 5

○ Step 7

Hint: Read all the steps in order.

5 After you finish painting, you should —

○ cover things.

○ buy more paint.

○ clean the brushes.

○ go to the paint store.

Hint: Read the last two steps.

TEST TIP

When you read directions, the order is very important. Imagine yourself following the steps in order. Questions 3, 4, and 5 all ask you about the order of events.

GO ON ⬛▶

SKILL 2: IDENTIFYING SUPPORTING IDEAS

The setting of a story lets you know when and where the story is taking place.

Fred Lamb had a dream to build the tallest building in the world. He wanted to put this building in New York City. Nobody had ever built such a tall building before.

All of the workers had to be very careful. They worked very hard and very long hours. They even worked at night. After six months they were done. In 1931, the Empire State Building was opened!

The Empire State Building was well built. In 1945, an airplane crashed into it. This did not knock it down.

Today, many people come to look at it. From the top, you can see for 80 miles. It is a wonderful place to visit!

1 **The story takes place in —**

○ Fred Lamb's home.

○ New York City.

○ a dream.

○ an airplane.

Hint: Read the first paragraph.

2 **The Empire State Building was built —**

○ hundreds of years ago.

○ last year.

○ in 1945.

○ in 1931.

Hint: Look at the second paragraph.

3 **The airplane crash took place —**

○ before the Empire State Building was done.

○ while Fred Lamb was dreaming.

○ after the Empire State Building was built.

○ while the people were working at night.

Hint: Look at the third paragraph.

GO ON ➡

The first train was built in England in 1825. It did not go very fast. It could not carry many people. Sometimes it did not work at all. But it was better than riding on horses.

4 **Where was the first train built?**

○ the United States

○ Canada

○ England

○ Mexico

Hint: Read the first sentence.

5 **When was the first train built?**

○ 1825

○ 1852

○ 1895

○ 1925

Hint: Look at the first sentence.

I set up the tent in the backyard. I had my sleeping bag and my pillow. I made sure I had enough food. I took out my flashlight. It was getting dark. Before long, it was time to go to bed.

6 **When is this story taking place?**

○ afternoon

○ night

○ morning

○ lunch time

Hint: Look at the last two sentences.

TEST TIP

Always read a test story carefully. Do not skip any sentences. There could be clues anywhere in the story.

The main idea is the meaning of a passage. Many times it is a sentence in the passage.

The earth goes around the sun. In winter, our part of the earth is farther away from the sun. It is very cold and it stays darker longer. In the summer, our part of the earth is closer to the sun. Then it is very warm.

1   **What is the main idea of this story?**

   ○ The earth moves around the sun.

   ○ It is cold in the winter.

   ○ It is darker in the winter.

   ○ It is warm in the summer.

   Hint: What does the whole story talk about?

Many people play soccer. It is played in every country. Soccer has been around for almost 3,000 years. Some people played soccer in China a long time ago. Then people started to play it in other countries. Soon, it was played all around the world.

2   **What is the main idea of this passage?**

   ○ Soccer has been played for almost 3,000 years.

   ○ Soccer is played by people all over the world.

   ○ Some people played soccer in China.

   ○ People started to play soccer in other countries.

   Hint: The first two sentences and the last sentence give you the main idea.

GO ON ▶

Hiking is a great way for you to have fun. All you need is a good pair of shoes. You can hike in many places, such as the woods or a valley. You can walk for a long or short time. Hiking is even better if you go with your friends.

3 **What is the main idea of this story?**

○ You need good hiking shoes.

○ You will have a good time hiking.

○ Hikes can be long or short.

○ You can hike in the woods.

Hint: What does the whole story talk about?

Mother's Day is a special day. There are many things you can do for your mother. You can make a pretty card or cook a nice meal. You can help clean the house or wash the clothes. It is a time to show your mother that you care.

4 **What is the main idea of this passage?**

○ You can cook a meal.

○ You can make a card.

○ You can help clean the house.

○ Mother's Day should be a special day.

Hint: Which choice is about the whole passage?

The winter in New York in 1994 was one to remember. There was a lot of snow. This made it hard for people to get around. Many schools were closed. It was also very cold. Many people were sick. People were glad when the winter was over.

5 **What is the main idea of this passage?**

○ The winter of 1994 was bad.

○ Many schools had to close.

○ People were sick.

○ It was hard to get around.

Hint: What does the whole story talk about?

TEST TIP

To find the main idea, ask yourself "What is this story about?" or "What is the big idea?"

GO ON➭

A good summary contains the main idea of a passage. It is short but includes the most important points.

Bats are different from many other animals. They are the only mammal that can fly. Some bats live in trees. Most bats live in caves or in attics. They only come out at night. When they are resting they hang upside down. Bats are very interesting animals.

1   **What is this mostly about?**

○   Most bats live in caves or attics.

○   Bats can fly.

○   Bats only come out at night.

○   Bats are interesting animals.

Hint: Which sentence tells you about the whole passage?

Have you ever gone to Boston? It is a great city. There are all kinds of boats to see and walk around on. There are places to visit where you can learn about science. There are many places to get great food. Boston is a wonderful place with many things to see and do!

2   **What is this mostly about?**

○   Boston is an interesting city to visit.

○   You can eat good food in Boston.

○   Boston has all kinds of boats to see.

○   There are places to learn about science.

Hint: Which sentence tells you about the whole passage?

GO ON ▶

There is a lot to learn about owls. Owls are awake at night. They can see very well in the dark. They can hunt for their food. They can also hear things moving in the dark. Owls sleep during the day. They sleep high up in trees. This keeps them safe.

3 What is this passage mostly about?

○ There are many things to learn about owls.

○ Owls sleep during the day.

○ Owls can see in the dark.

○ Owls sleep high up in trees.

Hint: Which sentence tells you about the whole passage?

Many children enjoy bowling. To play, you need to have a few things. The bowling ball has to fit your fingers. Next, you need a special pair of shoes just for bowling. Then, you are ready to bowl. Try to throw the ball straight. With some practice, you'll do fine!

4 Which sentence tells what this story is mostly about?

○ The ball should be just right.

○ Get the right kind of shoes.

○ To bowl you need some special things.

○ Few children enjoy bowling.

Hint: Which sentence tells you about the whole passage?

Jane Addams was a famous woman. She wanted to help poor people. Jane bought an old house. She fixed it up. Then, she started a school for children. At night, grownups came to learn. Jane Addams worked hard to help more and more people.

5 What is this passage mostly about?

○ Jane Addams fixed up an old house.

○ Jane Addams helped many people.

○ Jane Addams helped teach grownups.

○ Jane Addams liked children.

Hint: Which sentence tells you about the whole passage?

TEST TIP

Find the difference between answer choices. Every answer choice in question 5 begins with "Jane Addams." The words that come next make the answers different.

STOP

Knowing what happened (the <u>effect</u>) and what made it happen (the <u>cause</u>) helps you to understand what you read.

Jill could not run very fast. She could never win a race. She wanted to do better. So, every day after school she practiced running. After a while she ran faster and faster. When Jill ran in the next race, she won and was very happy!

1 Why couldn't Jill win a race at first?

○ She was not happy.

○ Jill ran in too many races.

○ She was not a fast runner.

○ Jill wanted to run fast.

Hint: Look at the first sentence.

2 Why did Jill win?

○ She practiced a lot.

○ She wanted to win.

○ She was very happy.

○ She went to school.

Hint: Look at the fourth sentence.

One day, Tony saw a beautiful plant growing in his yard. He wanted it to keep growing, so each day he watered it. He also pulled up the weeds near it. After two weeks, the plant grew even bigger. Soon, it had pretty flowers. Tony felt proud.

3 What caused the plant to grow bigger?

○ It was planted in Tony's yard.

○ It had weeds near it.

○ It grew pretty flowers.

○ Tony watered it.

Hint: What did Tony do to help the plant grow bigger?

4 Why was Tony proud?

○ He cared for the plant and it grew.

○ He saw a plant growing in the yard.

○ He waited for two weeks.

○ The flowers were pretty.

Hint: Reread the passage. Why would Tony feel proud of himself?

GO ON ➡

Long ago there lived a young woman named Margo. She lived all by herself in a house in the woods. Margo did not always like being alone. One day she found a little rabbit. The rabbit had hurt his leg. Margo felt sorry for it. She took the rabbit inside and took care of it. She gave the rabbit some lettuce to eat. The rabbit thanked Margo by licking her cheek. Margo named the rabbit Fluffy and kept it as a pet. Margo was no longer lonely.

5   Why did Margo bring the rabbit into her house?

○ She saw he was hungry.

○ She did not like to be alone.

○ She saw he was hurt.

○ She lived in the woods.

Hint: Margo brought in the rabbit. Why did she do this?

6   Why did the rabbit want to stay with Margo?

○ She took good care of him.

○ He wanted to eat more lettuce.

○ He saw Margo in the woods.

○ He did not want to be hurt.

Hint: The rabbit stayed with Margo. Why did he do this?

7   Why was Margo happy at the end of the story?

○ She did not like her house.

○ She liked to walk in the woods.

○ She wanted to find more rabbits.

○ She would not have to be alone.

Hint: Look at the last sentence. Why was Margo glad to have Fluffy?

TEST TIP

To check your answers, ask yourself, "Why did I choose this answer?"

GO ON ▶

SKILL 4: PERCEIVING RELATIONSHIPS AND RECOGNIZING OUTCOMES

Sometimes you can tell what might happen next. You must think about what would make sense if the story were to go on.

Luis came home from school. His mother told him to do his homework, but he did not want to. First, he had some milk and cookies. Then, he played with his toys. After dinner he drew some pictures. Soon, it was time to go to bed.

1   **What might happen to Luis the next day?**

○ He will not have his homework.

○ He will do well in school.

○ His mother will give him toys.

○ He will have milk and an apple.

Hint: What is most likely to happen the next day?

Miguel listened to the news. They said it will be very hot tomorrow. It will stay warm for the next few days. Miguel put his bathing suit on a chair. He was going to have fun.

2   **What will Miguel do tomorrow?**

○ sit on the chair

○ watch the news

○ go swimming

○ read a book

Hint: Read the whole paragraph.

Alicia asked to go to the bathroom. She ran down the hall. "No running in the hall," her teacher yelled. Alicia did not look where she was going. Just then, Herbie came out of his classroom. He was not looking where he was going.

3   **What will happen next?**

○ Alicia will return to her class.

○ Alicia and Herbie will bump into each other.

○ Alicia will say hello to Herbie.

○ Alicia's teacher will be happy.

Hint: You need to read the whole paragraph.

GO ON

Chuck and Fatima wanted to put on a magic show. They practiced for a long time. They wanted to make sure they could do the tricks. When they were ready, they invited all of their friends.

4 What is probably going to happen next?

○ Fatima will decide not to do the tricks.

○ No children will come to see the show.

○ Chuck and Fatima will have a magic show.

○ Their parents will come to the show.

Hint: Think about how Chuck and Fatima got ready. What will happen next?

TEST TIP

To answer question 4, find the answer that is most <u>likely</u> to happen.

Kyle got a new dog named Lucky. Kyle was teaching him to chase after a ball. The first time Kyle threw it, Lucky did not chase it. The next time Kyle threw the ball, he put a treat near it. Lucky went to get it. Pretty soon he did not need the treat.

5 What will Lucky do the next time the ball is thrown?

○ He will go get the ball.

○ He will want a treat.

○ Lucky will run away.

○ Kyle will have to get it.

Hint: Read the last two sentences to find out what Lucky will do.

Alma loved to read. One day, her father gave her some books. There were books about sports. Some books were about science. Others had fairy tales and scary stories. She put them away in her closet. The next day her teacher gave her a book report to do.

6 What is Alma likely to do next?

○ She will clean her closet.

○ She will take out a book and read.

○ She will ask for more books.

○ She will not want the books.

Hint: What is in Alma's closet?

SKILL 5: MAKING INFERENCES AND GENERALIZATIONS

The way a character acts tells you about that person's mood.

One day, Sam's parents had some news. "We are going to move to a new town! You will be going to a new school," his father said. Sam yelled, " I don't want to go. I won't have any friends!" His mother and father talked to Sam. They told him he would meet new people. He would make new friends. Now, Sam felt a little better.

1   How did Sam feel about the news?

○   He was mad because he did not want to move.

○   He felt glad because he wanted to make new friends.

○   He was upset because he did not like school.

○   He was excited about moving.

Hint: Read what Sam said to see how he felt.

Alex lives in Florida. It is always warm there. He went to visit his cousins in Maine. It was very cold and snowy. He had never seen snow before. He could not wait to play in it. After putting on some warm clothes, Alex ran outside and jumped in it. "This is great," he yelled. He laughed and kept on playing.

2   How do you think Alex felt?

○   angry

○   excited

○   bored

○   friendly

Hint: You must read the entire passage to find out how Alex felt.

GO ON

Laura was working hard on her book report. She wrote her report using her best writing. Now she was ready to make the cover. Just then, her mom called her for dinner. When she was finished eating, she saw that her little brother had ripped the report. Now she would have to start over.

3   How did Laura feel when she saw what her brother had done?

○ Laura was glad.

○ Laura was angry.

○ Laura was hungry.

○ Laura was thankful.

Hint: Read the whole passage. Think about the first and last sentences.

Ari wanted to buy his mother a birthday present. He saw a necklace that he knew she would love. It cost more money than he had. Ari had a plan. Every day after school, he looked for empty soda cans. He turned them in for five cents each. Soon he had enough money to buy the necklace.

4   How will Ari feel when he goes to buy the necklace?

○ brave

○ mad

○ proud

○ silly

Hint: Read the whole paragraph. Think about what Ari was now able to do.

TEST TIP

The answers to these questions are not stated in the stories. You need to think about what happens to find an answer. This is called <u>making inferences</u>.

Skill 6: Recognizing Points of View, Facts, and Opinions

It is important to know the difference between fact and opinion. A <u>fact</u> is real and an <u>opinion</u> states a feeling or belief. Words that describe state opinions.

Many children are afraid of sharks. They think sharks like to eat people. Most times, this is not true. Not all sharks want to hurt people. They really want to eat tiny plants and fish. You should not be afraid of sharks.

1   **Which of these is a FACT from the passage?**

○ Sharks are the best fish.

○ Most sharks eat plants and fish.

○ Sharks are pretty fish.

○ You should be afraid of sharks.

Hint: Words like "best," "pretty," and "should" are opinion words.

Maine is a great place to visit. There are very nice beaches. You can swim in the ocean. You can also walk in the woods. Some people like to climb the mountains. They can climb to the top and see far away. There is a lot to do in Maine.

2   **Which of these is NOT a fact from the passage?**

○ Maine is a great place to visit.

○ You can walk in the woods.

○ Some people climb mountains.

○ There are beaches.

Hint: Facts are real and true. Which sentence is an opinion?

GO ON ▶

Seals are in great danger. Some people hunt them for their thick fur. They use the fur to make warm coats. Other people hunt the seals for food. In some places, laws protect seals. Seals cannot be killed for any reason. We need more laws.

3   A fact from the passage is that seals

○ live in the water.

○ are in danger.

○ like to eat meat.

○ hunt people.

Hint: A fact is real and true.

Have you ever tried to high jump? High jumping can be a lot of fun. A bar rests across two poles. You have to jump over this. You run quickly up to the bar. If you are high enough, you will go over the bar.

4   Which of these is an opinion from the passage?

○ A bar rests across two poles.

○ High jumping can be a lot of fun.

○ You run quickly up to the bar.

○ You jump over the bar.

Hint: Words that describe are opinion words.

Many things happen when we eat. We chew the food into little pieces. This is so our bodies can use it. It travels down a tube into the stomach. It goes from there to other parts of the body. We all need to eat to live.

5   Which of these is a fact from the passage?

○ Food travels from the stomach to the mouth.

○ We swallow big pieces of food.

○ Food is used in many parts of our body.

○ We should not eat too often.

Hint: A fact is real and true. What is really said in the passage?

TEST TIP

The word <u>should</u> is often found in opinions. Read these two sentences:

• We sing every day.

• We should sing every day.

The second sentence is an opinion because it includes the word <u>should</u>.

 STOP

READING COMPREHENSION

Directions: Read each story carefully. Then read each question. Darken the circle for the correct answer, or write the answer on the lines.

> **TRY THIS** More than one answer choice may seem correct. Choose the answer that goes best with the story.

Sample A

Mr. Feld's Garden

Mr. Feld has a garden. Each day, he pulls out the weeds. He stays on his knees for a long time. Sometimes they hurt him. Today his son gave him some knee pads. Now Mr. Feld's knees won't hurt anymore.

What did Mr. Feld's son give him?

○ a watering can

○ a new rake

○ knee pads

○ some seeds

> **THINK IT THROUGH** The correct answer is knee pads. The next-to-last sentence says, "Today his son gave him some knee pads."

STOP

Katie and Josephine

Katie and Josephine were waiting for the bus. They looked up at the sky. Katie put on her raincoat. Josephine pulled up her hood. The bus came. They got in fast.

1 What were the girls doing?

○ playing football

○ waiting for the bus

○ waiting for the train

○ riding an airplane

2 Why did Katie and Josephine get into the bus fast?

_____

_____

_____

_____

GO ON

The Lion and the Mouse

A big, fierce lion was sleeping under a tree. A mouse ran up on the lion's back. Then the lion woke up, and he was angry at the mouse. He caught the mouse in his paw.

"Please do not eat me," said the mouse. "If you let me go, I will help you some time."

The lion thought the mouse was funny. "How could you help me?" he laughed. But then he let the mouse go.

Later that day the lion got caught in a hunter's net. He tried and tried to get free, but he could not get out of the net. The lion was ready to give up, but then he saw the mouse.

"Please help me," the lion said. The mouse began to chew on the net. Soon the net broke apart, and the lion was able to climb out of the net. The mouse had set the lion free.

3 **How did the mouse help the lion?**

○ She brought the lion food.

○ She found the lion's friends.

○ She fixed the lion's paw.

○ She chewed the net apart.

4 **The boxes below show things that happened in the story.**

The lion caught the mouse.		The mouse set the lion free.
1	2	3

What belongs in Box 2?

○ The lion was sleeping.

○ The mouse woke up the lion.

○ The lion let the mouse go.

○ The mouse ran up the lion's back.

5 **Why was the lion angry?**

_____

_____

_____

_____

_____

_____

_____

6 **Which of these lessons best fits the story?**

○ Little friends cannot help.

○ A mouse should not walk on a lion.

○ Little friends can be good friends.

○ Laughing makes you feel better.

GO ON ▶

A Letter to Harry

Dear Harry,

I wish you lived near me. We had the best costume party last night. It would have been more fun if you had been here. I dressed up like a cat. We invited all the kids on my street. Some of my friends from school came, too.

We had the party in the garage. I helped my dad fix it up. We hung colorful banners and streamers from the ceiling. My dad dressed up like a monster. We bobbed for apples in a big pail of water. The only way I could get one was to put my whole head under the water. I pushed the apple against the bottom of the pail and finally got it.

Later my dad made some special root beer. This is how he did it:

First, he put sugar into some water, and then he added root beer *extract.* That's the flavoring that makes it taste like root beer.

To finish, my dad stirred it and added lots of dry ice. When he poured in the dry ice, it made a lot of white smoke!

Chris had one of the best costumes. He was dressed like a hot dog. At the end of the party we helped Mom make popcorn.

What have you been doing? When are you going to come and visit? My mom says you can come anytime. We're going to Texas for New Year's Day. Write me soon.

Your friend,
Tom

GO ON ➤

7 **What is Tom's letter mostly about?**

   ◯ his party

   ◯ his class at school

   ◯ his costume

   ◯ his trip to Texas

8 **How does Tom feel about Harry?**

_____

_____

_____

_____

_____

9 **If you are making root beer, you should—**

   ◯ add sugar to flour.

   ◯ stir in butter.

   ◯ pour in milk.

   ◯ add sugar to water.

10 **What kind of party did Tom have?**

   ◯ a pizza party

   ◯ a birthday party

   ◯ a garden party

   ◯ a costume party

11 **In this story, Harry is the name of Tom's—**

   ◯ friend.

   ◯ teacher.

   ◯ uncle.

   ◯ neighbor.

12 **In this story, what does the word extract mean?**

   ◯ a kind of sugar

   ◯ a kind of flavoring

   ◯ a kind of nut

   ◯ a kind of flour

13 **When did Tom write the letter?**

   ◯ on a Monday

   ◯ during the summer

   ◯ the day after his party

   ◯ on New Year's Day

14 **Tom's letter does not tell—**

   ◯ where his friend Harry lives.

   ◯ what costume his dad wore.

   ◯ about bobbing for apples.

   ◯ where he is going for New Year's Day.

GO ON

Join Now!

This month is the time to join in and help others. Any second grader at Smith School can join in.

Read the list of things to do. Choose those you like best. Sign up on the sheet below by Thursday.

Ms. Salina will lead the activities. Students who do two or more things from the list this month will earn a volunteer pin.

To help others, we will:

1. Read to younger students.

2. Pick up litter at Travis Park.

3. Make greeting cards to send to a hospital.

4. Record songs on tape to send to a nursing home.

Your Name	Activity Numbers	Your Teacher's Name
Meg Klein	2, 4	Mr. Ward

15 **Who will earn a pin?**

○ all students who sign up

○ Ms. Salina's homeroom students

○ students who do at least two things from the list

○ students in the hospital

16 **Why would students volunteer?**

_____

_____

_____

_____

17 **After students sign up, what will probably happen next?**

○ Ms. Salina will speak to them.

○ They will sing songs.

○ They will get a volunteer pin.

○ They will go shopping.

18 **Which of the following is not listed on the sign-up sheet?**

○ your name

○ your room number

○ activity numbers

○ your teacher's name

GO ON ➡

A Great Play

Dawn had a part in the school play. She had to wear a costume. First, she put on a gray suit with a long tail. Then, she painted a pink circle on her nose. A pair of big gray ears finished the costume. It was time for her part. She walked onto the stage. A boy dressed like a cat crawled toward her. She grabbed a piece of cheese and ran. She was faster than the cat. Everyone laughed and laughed.

19 **Why did Dawn wear a costume?**

○ She was going to a party.

○ She was playing with friends.

○ She was in a school play.

○ She liked to dress up.

20 **What animal was Dawn most likely dressed as?**

○ an elephant

○ a dog

○ a cat

○ a mouse

21 **What is this story mostly about?**

○ Dawn's part in the school play

○ how to make costumes for plays

○ how to act in plays

○ animals in plays

22 **What could be another title for this story?**

_____

_____

_____

_____

_____

STOP

A sample question helps you to understand the type of question you will be asked in the test that follows.

Sample A

A Note for Ellen

Ellen's mother was going to be home late. She left a note for Ellen that said, "Please clean your room. Then you may read or watch television. I should be home about 4:00."

What should Ellen do first?

○ clean her room

○ watch television

○ read

○ call her friends

Growing Flowers

To grow flowers, do the following:

1. Put dirt in a pot.
2. Place flower seeds in the pot.
3. Cover the seeds with more dirt.
4. Put the pot in the sun.
5. Water the seeds, and wait for the flowers to grow!

1   What is the last thing you should do?

○ cover the seeds with dirt

○ put dirt in the pot

○ buy seeds

○ water the seeds

2   What is the best way to find out more about growing flowers?

○ Read a book about gardening.

○ Put cut flowers in a vase.

○ Draw pictures of flowers.

○ Sit in the sun.

3   To grow flowers you will need—

○ a shovel.

○ seeds.

○ gloves.

○ a spoon.

4   Where should you put the pot?

_____

_____

_____

_____

_____

GO ON ➡

All About Owls

Did you know that owls are good hunters? Owls sleep all day long. At night they wake up and fly around. They look for mice to eat. Owls have very big eyes. Big eyes let in more light. Owls can see better at night than we can. Owls also hear very well. They can hear a mouse running in the grass. They can fly without making any noise at all. All these things make owls good hunters.

5 This story does <u>not</u> tell—

- ○ the kind of eyes owls have.
- ○ what makes owls good hunters.
- ○ about different kinds of owls.
- ○ what owls like to eat.

6 This story was written mainly to—

- ○ ask you to join a club.
- ○ explain how important sleep is for good health.
- ○ tell about a kind of bird.
- ○ describe what animals do at night.

7 A special thing about the owl is that it can fly very—

- ○ quietly.   ○ loudly.
- ○ quickly.   ○ high in the air.

8 Why can owls see better at night?

_____

_____

_____

_____

_____

9 When do owls sleep?

- ○ at night
- ○ during the afternoon
- ○ through the morning
- ○ all day

GO ON ➡

A Scary Walk

"What a great day for a walk!" John said. He could hear the birds singing. John was glad that he had made this trip to the mountains. After breakfast John took off, whistling a tune. The trail went up the mountain. He walked for a while, and then he looked for a rock to rest on. John was tired. "What a mountain man I turned out to be!" he said.

While he rested, John looked around. Suddenly he saw the opening to a cave. It was big enough to walk through. "I wonder how deep it is," he said. "I wonder if there are any cave drawings! I guess the only way to find out is to see for myself."

At first John had no trouble seeing in the cave. He went around a bend. He lit a match. "Just a little farther," he said to himself. Suddenly his match went out! He lit another one. But now things looked strange. John was lost!

When his second match went out, John got really frightened. Then he thought he heard a scratching noise. John struck his last match. In the light he saw hundreds of bats hanging on the cave walls! Their eyes glittered red. John started screaming and running as fast as he could. Luckily for John, he was running in the right direction. He ran all the way back to his camp.

10 **What did John hear when he started his walk?**

- ○ water running
- ○ bats scratching
- ○ dogs barking
- ○ birds singing

11 **What will John probably do next?**

_____

_____

_____

_____

_____

_____

12 **What is this story mostly about?**

- ○ bats hanging on cave walls
- ○ John's adventure in a cave
- ○ using matches wisely
- ○ hiking safety

13 **Why did John go into the cave?**

- ○ He liked caves.
- ○ He wanted to see what was inside the cave.
- ○ He was looking for a friend.
- ○ It started to rain.

14 **These boxes show things that happened in the story.**

John rested on a rock.		John saw hundreds of bats.
1	2	3

What belongs in Box 2?

- ○ John ran back to camp.
- ○ John walked up the mountain.
- ○ John got lost in a cave.
- ○ John ate breakfast.

15 **How did John feel when he saw the bats?**

- ○ interested
- ○ angry
- ○ frightened
- ○ sad

16 **This story is most like a—**

- ○ poem.
- ○ true story.
- ○ fairy tale.
- ○ tall tale.

17 **Another name for this story could be—**

- ○ "Mountain Man"
- ○ "Finding Cave Drawings"
- ○ "John's Surprise"
- ○ "How to Explore Caves"

STOP

READING VOCABULARY

UNDERSTANDING WORD MEANINGS

Directions: Darken the circle for the word or words that have the <u>same</u> or <u>almost the same</u> meaning as the underlined word.

> **TRY THIS** Choose your answer carefully. Some choices may seem correct. Be sure to think about the meaning of the underlined word.

Sample A

To <u>raise</u> something is to—

- ○ lift it
- ○ count it
- ○ fly it
- ○ open it

> **THINK IT THROUGH** The correct answer is <u>lift it</u>. If you raise something, you lift it up. To raise something is not to count it, fly it, or open it.

STOP

1 To <u>choose</u> is to—
- ○ hide
- ○ check
- ○ color
- ○ pick

2 A <u>blizzard</u> is most like a—
- ○ thunderstorm
- ○ snowstorm
- ○ river
- ○ movie

3 To <u>shout</u> is to—
- ○ jump
- ○ slip
- ○ yell
- ○ skip

4 <u>Least</u> means—
- ○ best
- ○ closest
- ○ smallest
- ○ fastest

5 A <u>pail</u> is most like a—
- ○ bucket
- ○ pain
- ○ house
- ○ hill

6 Something that is moving <u>forward</u> is going—
- ○ back
- ○ ahead
- ○ behind
- ○ over

STOP

Directions: Darken the circle beside the sentence that uses the underlined word in the same way as the sentence in the box, or write the answer on the blank lines.

> **TRY THIS**
>
> Read the sentence in the box. Decide what the underlined word means. Then find the sentence with the underlined word that has the same meaning.

Sample A

> Have you ever seen a two-dollar <u>bill</u>?

In which sentence does <u>bill</u> mean the same as it does in the sentence above?

○ I paid with two quarters and one dollar <u>bill</u>.

○ Uncle Carl got a <u>bill</u> for the newspaper.

○ A parrot has a big <u>bill</u>.

○ The store will <u>bill</u> us for these shoes.

> **THINK IT THROUGH**
>
> The correct answer is the <u>first sentence, I paid with two quarters and one dollar bill</u>. In this sentence and the sentence in the box, bill means "a type of money."

STOP

---

1 | The sun's <u>light</u> is bright.

In which sentence does <u>light</u> mean the same as it does in the sentence above?

○ Will you <u>light</u> the candles?

○ The <u>light</u> from the flashlight helped us to see.

○ That bag is <u>light</u>, not heavy.

○ Pink is a <u>light</u> color.

2 | It is Tia's turn to <u>ring</u> the bell.

Use <u>ring</u> in a sentence. It should have the same meaning as it does in the sentence in the box.

_____

_____

_____

_____

_____

_____

STOP

Directions: Darken the circle for the word or words that give the meaning of the underlined word, or write the answer on the blank lines.

TRY THIS

Read the first sentence carefully. Look for clue words in the sentence to help you. Then use each answer choice in place of the underlined word. Remember that the underlined word and your answer must have the same meaning.

Sample A

The magician made the rabbit <u>vanish</u> from our sight. <u>Vanish</u> means—

○ jump   ○ disappear

○ shine   ○ smile

THINK IT THROUGH The correct answer is **disappear**. <u>Vanish</u> means to no longer be seen. All four choices are things a magician could make a rabbit do. But only <u>disappear</u> has the same meaning as vanish.

STOP

1 Singing, talking loudly, or whistling is <u>forbidden</u> in the library. What does <u>forbidden</u> mean?

_____

_____

_____

_____

_____

2 The artist made a quick pencil <u>sketch</u> of the village. <u>Sketch</u> means—

○ drawing   ○ song

○ story   ○ fence

3 Melissa plans to <u>save</u> money so she will be able to buy some new skates. <u>Save</u> means—

○ keep

○ bet

○ pay

○ find

4 He <u>shoved</u> the frightened actor onto the stage. <u>Shoved</u> means—

○ sang

○ returned

○ pushed

○ read

STOP

Directions: Darken the circle under the compound word.

TRY THIS Look carefully at each word. Then look for the word that is made up of two words put together.

Sample A

carrot   harbor   herself
 ◯   ◯   ◯

THINK IT THROUGH Herself is a compound word made up of the words her and self. Each of these words can stand alone. Harbor and carrot are not made up of two words put together.

STOP

1	mailbox	listen	drawing	5	anyway	making	after
	◯	◯	◯		◯	◯	◯

2	closet	airplane	fasten	6	inches	someone	teacher
	◯	◯	◯		◯	◯	◯

3	football	looked	backing	7	fiddle	rather	bedroom
	◯	◯	◯		◯	◯	◯

4	pencil	follow	outside	8	bottle	bluebird	hundred
	◯	◯	◯		◯	◯	◯

STOP

Directions: Darken the circle under the word that shows the correct plural noun. A plural noun names more than one thing.

TRY THIS	Add –s to make many plural nouns. Add –es to make other plural nouns. Some plurals do not follow this pattern.

Sample A
more than one <u>couch</u>

THINK IT THROUGH	The correct answer is <u>couches</u>. Add –es to most nouns that end in <u>sh</u>, <u>ch</u>, or <u>x</u>.

couchs   couches   couch
○   ○   ○

STOP

1   more than one <u>house</u>

housees   housies   houses
○   ○   ○

5   more than one <u>star</u>

starrs   stars   stares
○   ○   ○

2   more than one <u>chair</u>

chair   chairs   chaires
○   ○   ○

6   more than one <u>mouse</u>

mouses   mousies   mice
○   ○   ○

3   more than one <u>puppy</u>

puppys   puppes   puppies
○   ○   ○

7   more than one <u>flower</u>

flowers   flowes   floweres
○   ○   ○

4   more than one <u>stitch</u>

stitches   stitchies   stitchs
○   ○   ○

8   more than one <u>man</u>

mans   manes   men
○   ○   ○

STOP

Directions: Darken the circle under the word that has the same sound or sounds as the underlined part of the first word in each row.

TRY THIS	Say the first word to yourself. Decide how the underlined part of the word sounds. Then as you say each answer choice, listen for that sound.

Sample A

n<u>o</u>se

low   night   loop
○   ○   ○

THINK IT THROUGH	<u>Low</u> is the correct answer. The "o" in low makes the same sound as the "o" in <u>nose</u>.

STOP

1   **<u>th</u>ere**

this   think   thin
○   ○   ○

2   **l<u>ou</u>d**

through   lid   cow
○   ○   ○

3   **bu<u>tt</u>er**

mother   bunny   writing
○   ○   ○

4   **qui<u>lt</u>**

mall   wilt   queen
○   ○   ○

5   **<u>c</u>ute**

pulling   luck   noon
○   ○   ○

6   **<u>rare</u>**

rain   fair   rough
○   ○   ○

7   **<u>c</u>at**

city   kitten   hat
○   ○   ○

8   **<u>st</u>ep**

desk   fast   teach
○   ○   ○

STOP

Directions: Darken the circle under the word that rhymes with the first word in each row.

TRY THIS

Say the first word to yourself. Listen to the sounds at the end of the word. Then say each answer choice. Listen for the word that ends with the same sounds. Rhyming words end with the same vowel and consonant sounds. The spellings can be different.

Sample A

more

fear   mow   for
○   ○   ○

THINK IT THROUGH

The correct answer is <u>for</u>. The words <u>more</u> and <u>for</u> rhyme. <u>Fear</u> ends with an <u>r</u> sound, but the vowel sound is different.

STOP

1. **new**

    newt   now   two
    ○   ○   ○

2. **red**

    said   real   seed
    ○   ○   ○

3. **mop**

    top   tip   tap
    ○   ○   ○

4. **ride**

    ray   cried   rice
    ○   ○   ○

5. **moon**

    foot   moo   June
    ○   ○   ○

6. **rain**

    rake   lane   paint
    ○   ○   ○

7. **four**

    dry   fork   poor
    ○   ○   ○

8. **own**

    now   phone   noon
    ○   ○   ○

STOP

Directions: Darken the circle for the word or words that have the <u>same</u> or <u>almost the same</u> meaning as the underlined word.

1 <u>Hardly</u> means—

○ a lot

○ not at all

○ more than

○ barely

2 To <u>begin</u> is to—

○ start

○ end

○ laugh

○ think

3 A <u>bundle</u> is a—

○ supper

○ mitten

○ bunch

○ bread

4 If something <u>sparkles</u>, it—

○ shines

○ bothers

○ pays

○ wins

Directions: Darken the circle beside the sentence that uses the underlined word in the same way as the sentence in the box, or write the answer on the blank lines.

5 | What <u>time</u> does the show start? |

In which sentence does <u>time</u> mean the same as it does in the sentence above?

○ I will <u>time</u> my brother's race.

○ We kept <u>time</u> with the music.

○ Everyone had a good <u>time</u>.

○ It's <u>time</u> for lunch.

6 | Did you feel a <u>drop</u> of rain? |

In which sentence does <u>drop</u> mean the same as it does in the sentence above?

○ I put the letter in the mail <u>drop</u>.

○ Please wipe up the <u>drop</u> of paint.

○ Leon's mom will <u>drop</u> us off.

○ Don't <u>drop</u> that glass!

GO ON

7 | Exercise is the <u>key</u> to good health.

In which sentence does <u>key</u> mean the same as it does in the sentence above?

○ A <u>key</u> on the piano is stuck.

○ I lost my <u>key</u> to the front door.

○ In what <u>key</u> are you singing?

○ Tim found the <u>key</u> to solving the puzzle.

8 | We planted flowers <u>last</u> spring.

Write a sentence in which <u>last</u> means the same as it does in the sentence above.

_____

_____

_____

_____

9 | Did you find the <u>iron</u> pot?

In which sentence does <u>iron</u> mean the same as it does in the sentence above?

○ The <u>iron</u> horseshoe is strong.

○ Lisa needs to <u>iron</u> her dress.

○ <u>Iron</u> out your differences.

○ Did you plug in the <u>iron</u>?

Directions: Darken the circle beside the word that gives the meaning of the underlined word.

10 We made a star <u>pattern</u> with beads. <u>Pattern</u> means—

○ circle

○ design

○ necklace

○ string

11 A family finally moved into the house that had been <u>vacant</u> for months. <u>Vacant</u> means—

○ white

○ empty

○ burned

○ filled

12 He painted <u>bold</u> colors next to soft ones. <u>Bold</u> means—

○ dull

○ bright

○ mixed

○ quiet

STOP

Directions: Darken the circle under the compound word.

13 frying   mitten   raincoat
    ○   ○   ○

14 notebook   other   parent
    ○   ○   ○

15 fresher   bathtub   bottle
    ○   ○   ○

16 wisdom   upstairs   artist
    ○   ○   ○

17 finger   grassy   birthday
    ○   ○   ○

18 remain   sidewalk   happen
    ○   ○   ○

Directions: Darken the circle under the word that shows the correct plural noun.

19 more than one tree
    trees   tree   tries
    ○   ○   ○

20 more than one bone
    bons   bonies   bones
    ○   ○   ○

21 more than one wish
    wishs   wishes   wishies
    ○   ○   ○

22 more than one baby
    babys   babies   babyes
    ○   ○   ○

23 more than one child
    children   childs   childes
    ○   ○   ○

24 more than one bear
    beares   berries   bears
    ○   ○   ○

GO ON ▶

Directions: Darken the circle under the word that has the same sound or sounds as the underlined part of the first word in each row.

Directions: Darken the circle under the word that rhymes with the first word in each row.

25 rea**ch**

shore   rink   chip
○   ○   ○

31 sip

lid   lap   lip
○   ○   ○

26 **c**enter

crate   loose   inch
○   ○   ○

32 green

grow   grin   mean
○   ○   ○

27 p**i**ne

pitch   peach   tie
○   ○   ○

33 blue

black   shoe   broom
○   ○   ○

28 **p**ie

fine   car   mop
○   ○   ○

34 fry

high   friend   hurry
○   ○   ○

29 fl**a**t

flew   apple   west
○   ○   ○

35 whale

hole   hill   pail
○   ○   ○

30 **ro**ast

grow   spoon   ripe
○   ○   ○

36 tune

food   noon   too
○   ○   ○

STOP

MATH PROBLEM-SOLVING PLAN

OVERVIEW

THE PROBLEM-SOLVING PLAN

Here are the steps to solve problems:

STEP 1: WHAT IS THE QUESTION?

Read the problem. Can you see what you must find? What is the question?

STEP 2: FIND THE FACTS

Find the facts:

    A. KEY FACTS are the facts you need to solve the problem.

    B. FACTS YOU DON'T NEED are those facts that are not needed to solve the problem.

    C. ARE MORE FACTS NEEDED? Do you need more facts to solve the problem?

STEP 3: CHOOSE A WAY TO SOLVE

Plan a way to solve the problem.

STEP 4: SOLVE

Use your plan to solve the problem.

STEP 5: DOES YOUR RESPONSE MAKE SENSE?

Write your answer in a complete sentence.
Read the problem again.
Does your answer make sense?

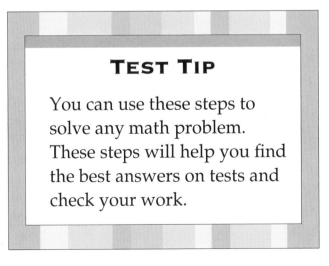

TEST TIP

You can use these steps to solve any math problem. These steps will help you find the best answers on tests and check your work.

Directions: Use the problem-solving plan to solve this math problem.

PROBLEM/QUESTION:

A store sells apples. The first apple costs 25¢. Each apple after that costs 20¢. If Paul buys 3 apples, how much does he pay?

STEP 1: WHAT IS THE QUESTION/GOAL?

_____

_____

_____

STEP 2: FIND THE FACTS

_____

_____

_____

STEP 3: SELECT A STRATEGY

_____

_____

_____

STEP 4: SOLVE

_____

_____

_____

STEP 5: DOES YOUR RESPONSE MAKE SENSE?

_____

_____

_____

_____

_____

Directions: Use the problem-solving plan to solve this math problem.

PROBLEM/QUESTION:

Jenny said, "I am thinking of a number. The number is less than 9 and greater than 5. It is an odd number." Name the number.

STEP 1: WHAT IS THE QUESTION/GOAL?

_____

_____

_____

STEP 2: FIND THE FACTS

_____

_____

_____

STEP 3: SELECT A STRATEGY

_____

_____

_____

STEP 4: SOLVE

_____

_____

_____

STEP 5: DOES YOUR RESPONSE MAKE SENSE?

_____

_____

_____

_____

_____

MATH PROBLEM SOLVING

Directions: Darken the circle for the correct answer, or write the answer on the lines.

Sample A

Which number shows the correct way to write three hundred plus fifty?

300 + 50

| 300 | 3,050 | 350 | 30,050 |
| ○ | ○ | ○ | ○ |

> **THINK IT THROUGH** Think about which numbers stand for ones, tens, and hundreds. The correct answer is <u>350</u>. This is the only number that equals 300 + 50.

STOP

1 Write the number that is in the hundreds place.

903 _____

2 Which shirt shows an even number?

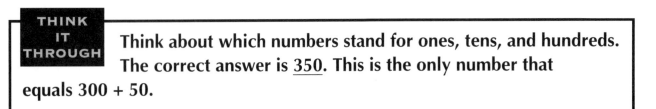

| 9 | 5 | 3 | 6 |
| ○ | ○ | ○ | ○ |

3 Which number tells the total number of carrots?

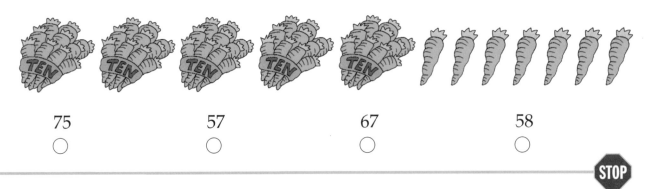

| 75 | 57 | 67 | 58 |
| ○ | ○ | ○ | ○ |

STOP

Directions: Darken the circle for the correct answer, or write the answer on the lines.

Sample A

Which shape is NOT divided into four equal pieces, or fourths?

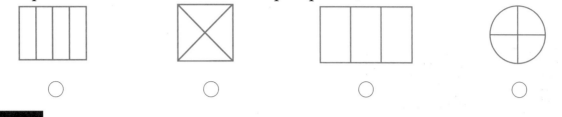

○   ○   ○   ○

 THINK IT THROUGH | **Look at the pictures. How many parts do you see in each picture? Find the picture that does NOT show fourths. The correct answer is the <u>third</u> shape. All the other shapes are divided into fourths.**

STOP

1 Six kittens are in the basket. Two kittens are outside the basket. Which number sentence describes the total number of kittens?

    ○   6 + 2 = 8   ○   10 − 2 = 8

    ○   6 − 2 = 4   ○   8 + 2 = 10

2 Which picture shows that one of the three apples has been eaten?

3 Write the number that makes this number sentence correct.

8 + □ = 8

_____

4 Which number makes this number sentence correct?

18 + □ = 21 + 18

  39   21   18   3

  ○   ○   ○   ○

STOP

Directions: Darken the circle for the correct answer, or write the answer on the lines.

Sample A

Which number is missing in this pattern? Find the number that belongs on the door that does not have a number.

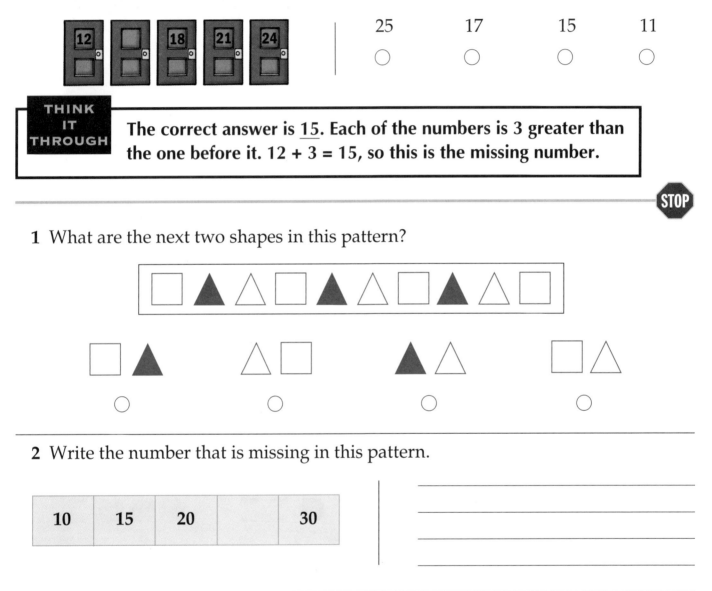

	25	17	15	11
	○	○	○	○

THINK IT THROUGH The correct answer is <u>15</u>. Each of the numbers is 3 greater than the one before it. 12 + 3 = 15, so this is the missing number.

STOP

1 What are the next two shapes in this pattern?

○   ○   ○   ○

2 Write the number that is missing in this pattern.

10	15	20		30

_____

_____

_____

_____

3 Max counted these birds. He started with 62. Which bird did Max count as number 71?

62   63   64   ○   ○   ○   ○

STOP

Directions: Darken the circle for the correct answer, or write the answer on the lines.

Sample A

Ann made this tally chart. Which picture shows the shell that Ann found six of?

Sand dollar	Conch	Whelk	Scallop
ᚷᚷ ///	////	ᚷᚷ /	///

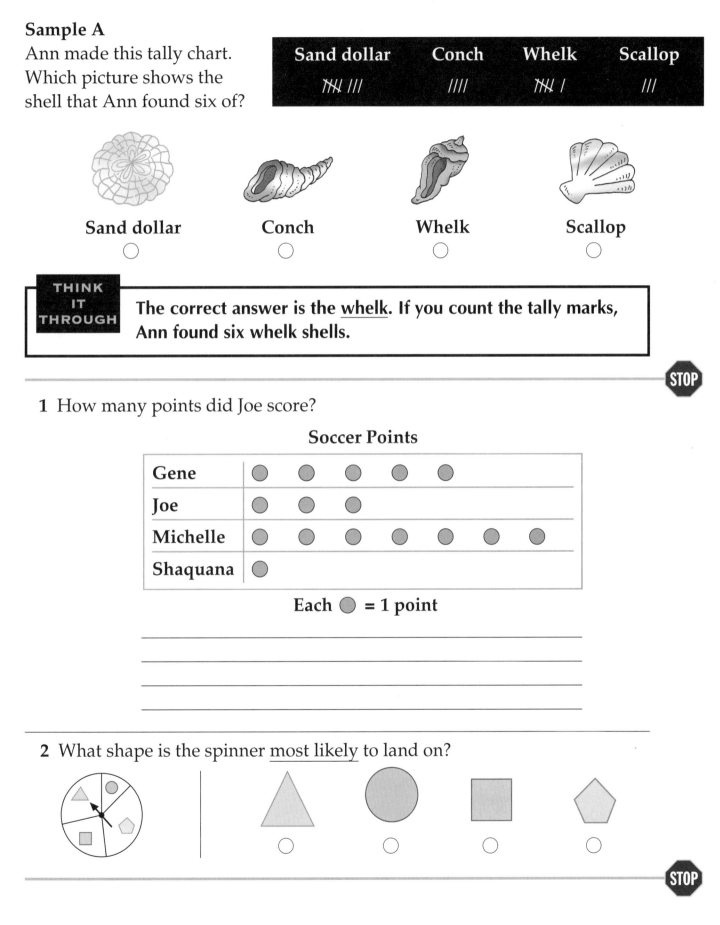

Sand dollar ○   Conch ○   Whelk ○   Scallop ○

THINK IT THROUGH The correct answer is the <u>whelk</u>. If you count the tally marks, Ann found six whelk shells.

STOP

1 How many points did Joe score?

Soccer Points

Gene	● ● ● ● ●
Joe	● ● ●
Michelle	● ● ● ● ● ● ●
Shaquana	●

Each ● = 1 point

_____

_____

_____

_____

2 What shape is the spinner <u>most likely</u> to land on?

△ ○   ● ○   ■ ○   ⬠ ○

STOP

Directions: Darken the circle for the correct answer.

Sample A

Think about folding each shape on the dotted line. Which shape has parts that will match exactly when you fold on the dotted line?

○   ○   ○   ○

THINK IT THROUGH   **The correct answer is the third figure. If you fold this figure on the dotted line, each side will be the same.**

STOP

1 Which box shows two triangles?

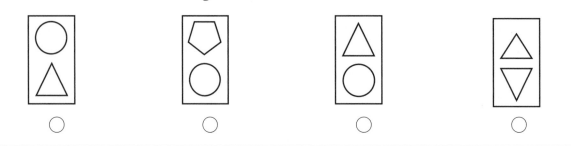

○   ○   ○   ○

2 Which shape has the same number of sides as the first shape in the row?

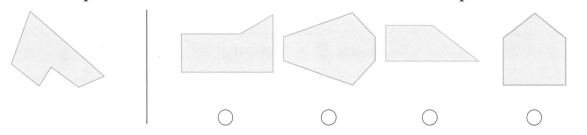

○   ○   ○   ○

3 Which card shows what the first card in the row looks like upside down?

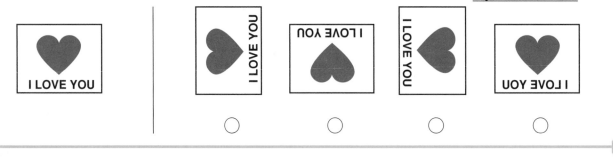

○   ○   ○   ○

STOP

Directions: Darken the circle for the correct answer, or write the answer on the lines.

Sample A

Sue has some coins. Which number shows how much money Sue will have left if she buys the banana?

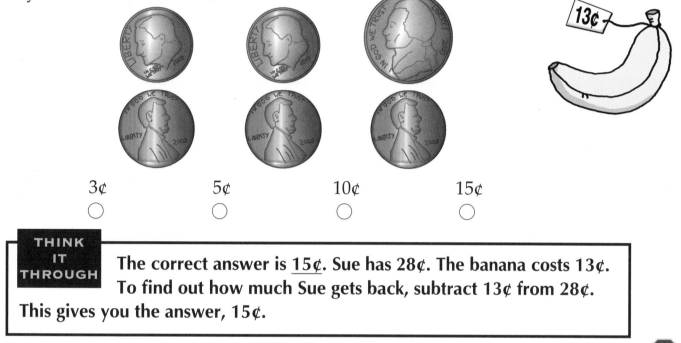

3¢	5¢	10¢	15¢
○	○	○	○

THINK IT THROUGH

The correct answer is 15¢. Sue has 28¢. The banana costs 13¢. To find out how much Sue gets back, subtract 13¢ from 28¢. This gives you the answer, 15¢.

STOP

1 Use a centimeter ruler. How long is this key in centimeters?

_____

_____

_____

_____

2 What unit would you use to measure the weight of a dog?

Kilometers	Pounds	Inches	Grams
○	○	○	○

3 What day is August 13 on this calendar?

August

Sun	Mon	Tues	Wed	Thur	Fri	Sat
			1	2	3	4
5	6	7	8	9	10	11
12	13	14	15	16	17	18
19	20	21	22	23	24	25
26	27	28	29	30	31	

○ Monday   ○ Friday

○ Tuesday   ○ Saturday

STOP

Directions: Darken the circle for the correct answer, or write the answer on the lines.

Sample A

Mrs. Chong bought 12 flowers. She put 8 of the flowers in a vase. Which number sentence shows how to find the number of flowers Mrs. Chong has left?

- ○ $12 + 8 = \Box$
- ○ $12 - 8 = \Box$
- ○ $12 + 4 = \Box$
- ○ $12 - \Box = 6$

THINK IT THROUGH The correct answer is 12 – 8. The clue words, "has left," tell you to subtract. Mrs. Chong has 12 flowers and puts 8 in a vase, so 12 – 8 is the number sentence that answers the question.

STOP

1 Nathan had three fish. He bought nine more. Which number sentence shows how to find how many fish Nathan has altogether?

- ○ $9 - 3 = \Box$
- ○ $12 - 9 = \Box$
- ○ $3 + 9 = \Box$
- ○ $3 + \Box = 9$

2 Sue thinks of one of these numbers. Her number is less than 35. The sum of the digits is 11. What is Sue's number?

| 38 | 34 | 29 | 24 |
| ○ | ○ | ○ | ○ |

3 Tia's age is between 31 and 41. The sum of the digits is 5. How old is Tia?

_____

_____

_____

_____

4 Lou thinks of one of these numbers. His number is inside the square and inside the triangle. It is even. What is Lou's number?

| 2 | 5 | 6 | 8 |
| ○ | ○ | ○ | ○ |

STOP

Directions: Darken the circle for the correct answer. If the correct answer is not given, darken the circle for NH (Not Here). If there are no choices, write the answer on the blank lines.

Sample A

It is Soon-Li's birthday. She gets nine presents from her friends. She gets five presents from her family. How many presents does she get?

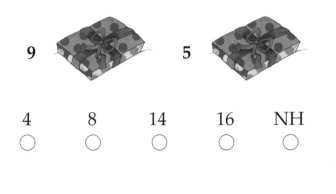

9   5

4   8   14   16   NH
○   ○   ○   ○   ○

THINK IT THROUGH The correct answer is the third answer choice, 14. She gets 9 presents from her friends and 5 from her family. The word <u>altogether</u> tells you to add. So there are 14 presents altogether, because 9 + 5 = 14.

 STOP

---

1 An art gallery has 60 pictures in the first room. There are 34 pictures in the second room. How many pictures are there in all?

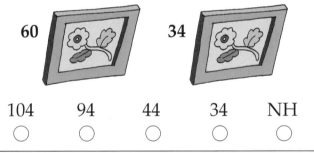

60   34

104   94   44   34   NH
○   ○   ○   ○   ○

2 There were five boats on the lake. Three more boats joined them. How many boats were there altogether?

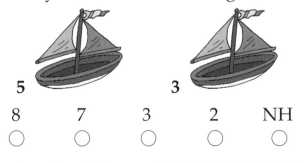

5   3

8   7   3   2   NH
○   ○   ○   ○   ○

3 The school served 56 bowls of chicken soup and 24 bowls of vegetable soup. How many bowls of soup did the school serve in all?

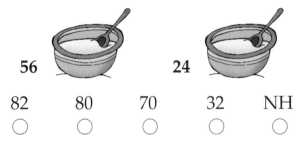

56   24

82   80   70   32   NH
○   ○   ○   ○   ○

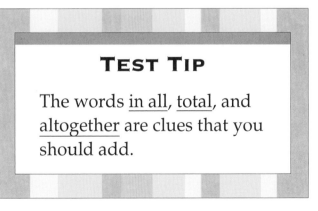

TEST TIP

The words <u>in all</u>, <u>total</u>, and <u>altogether</u> are clues that you should add.

GO ON ➡

4 A plane carries 18 large suitcases and 7 small suitcases. How many suitcases does the plane carry?

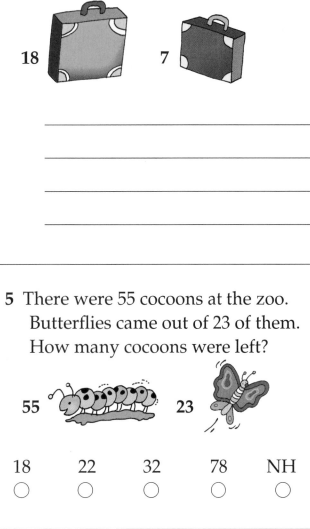

18   7

_____

_____

_____

_____

5 There were 55 cocoons at the zoo. Butterflies came out of 23 of them. How many cocoons were left?

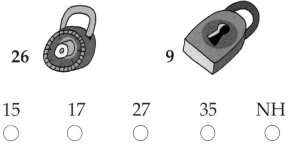

55   23

| 18 | 22 | 32 | 78 | NH |
| ○ | ○ | ○ | ○ | ○ |

6 A hardware store has 26 padlocks with dials and 9 locks with keys. How many more padlocks than key locks does the store have?

26   9

| 15 | 17 | 27 | 35 | NH |
| ○ | ○ | ○ | ○ | ○ |

7 There were 53 ribbons given at the county dog show. The judges gave 23 ribbons in the morning. How many ribbons did they give in the afternoon?

53   23

| 40 | 33 | 23 | 20 | NH |
| ○ | ○ | ○ | ○ | ○ |

8 Pat's Pizza Parlor sold 41 sausage-and-mushroom pizzas. It sold 12 plain sausage pizzas. How many more sausage-and-mushroom than plain mushroom pizzas did it sell?

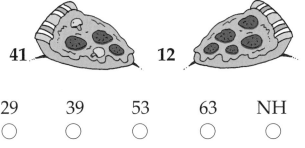

41   12

| 29 | 39 | 53 | 63 | NH |
| ○ | ○ | ○ | ○ | ○ |

TEST TIP

The words <u>how many more</u> are a clue that you should subtract. Subtract the smaller number from the larger number.

GO ON ➡

9 The garden center has 123 plants. It sells 47 plants. How many plants are left?

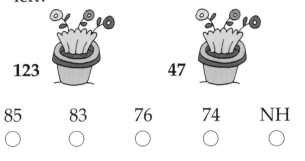

123   **47**

85   83   76   74   NH
○   ○   ○   ○   ○

10 Twelve clowns wear round hats. Nine clowns wear pointed hats. How many more clowns wear round hats?

12   **9**

21   13   11   3   NH
○   ○   ○   ○   ○

11 A fire station collects 207 toys. It gives 66 toys away. How many toys are left?

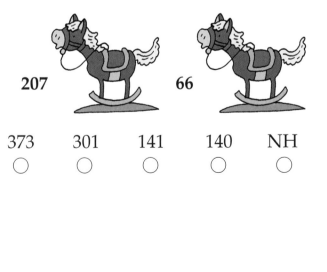

207   **66**

373   301   141   140   NH
○   ○   ○   ○   ○

12 An ice cream store sold 82 cones and 47 sundaes. How many more cones than sundaes did the store sell?

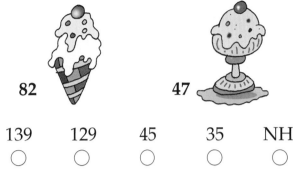

82   **47**

139   129   45   35   NH
○   ○   ○   ○   ○

13 Koji collects cars and trucks. He has 126 cars and 71 trucks. How many cars and trucks does he have altogether?

126   **71**

_____

_____

_____

_____

14 Jacob has a herd of goats. He has 30 brown goats and 16 white goats. How many more brown goats than white goats does Jacob have?

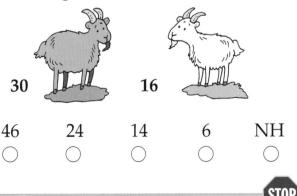

30   **16**

46   24   14   6   NH
○   ○   ○   ○   ○

STOP

Directions: Darken the circle for the correct answer. If the correct answer is not given, darken the circle for NH (Not Here). If there are no circles, write the answer on the lines.

TRY THIS

Study the problem carefully. Decide if you need to add or subtract. Then work the problem on scratch paper.

Sample A

$$17$$
$$- 9$$

6	8	26	28	NH
○	○	○	○	○

THINK IT THROUGH

The correct answer is <u>8</u>. 17 – 9 = 8. The second answer choice is correct because you can check your answer by adding the 9 and the 8, which gives you 17.

STOP

1

$$410$$
$$+ 62$$

482	472	358	348	NH
○	○	○	○	○

2   13 – 8 = ☐

8	7	6	5	NH
○	○	○	○	○

3   5 + 2 + 9 = ☐

17	16	15	14	NH
○	○	○	○	○

4   24 + 13 = ☐

11	21	37	47	NH
○	○	○	○	○

5   8 + 7 = ☐

1	14	16	25	NH
○	○	○	○	○

6

$$51$$
$$- 17$$

_____

_____

_____

_____

STOP

Directions: Darken the circle for the correct answer. If the correct answer is not given, darken the circle NH (Not Here). If there are no circles, write the answer on the lines.

1 There were 13 bees in a garden. Six bees flew away. How many bees were left?

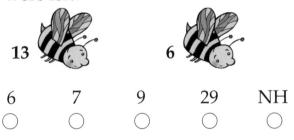

13   6

6	7	9	29	NH
○	○	○	○	○

2 Mr. Lopez picks 27 apples on Monday. He picks 8 apples on Tuesday. How many apples does he pick in all?

27   8

_____

_____

_____

3 Anton went to the zoo. He saw eight giraffes in the morning and three more in the afternoon. How many giraffes did Anton see?

8   3

4	6	11	15	NH
○	○	○	○	○

4 Keesha grew 32 red roses and 16 yellow roses. How many roses did Keesha grow?

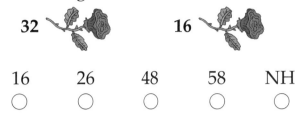

32   16

16	26	48	58	NH
○	○	○	○	○

5 What number makes this number sentence true?

$$7 + 5 = \square$$

12	11	3	2	NH
○	○	○	○	○

6 Lina works at a hot dog stand. She cooked 80 hot dogs. She sold 67 hot dogs. How many hot dogs does she have left?

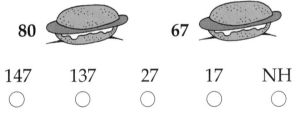

80   67

147	137	27	17	NH
○	○	○	○	○

7 Bob collects comic books. He had 614 comic books. Then he bought 44 more comic books. How many comic books does he have in all?

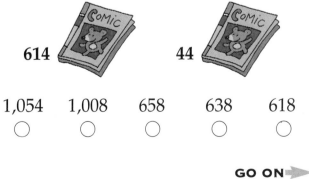

614   44

1,054	1,008	658	638	618
○	○	○	○	○

GO ON ⮕

8
$$14$$
$$\underline{-\ 8}$$

22	12	7	6	NH
○	○	○	○	○

9 $39 + 20 = \square$

69	59	29	19	NH
○	○	○	○	○

10
$$76$$
$$\underline{+\ 8}$$

68	74	78	84	NH
○	○	○	○	○

11
$$25$$
$$10$$
$$\underline{+\ 13}$$

58	52	48	38	NH
○	○	○	○	○

12
$$61$$
$$\underline{-\ 35}$$

26	36	86	96	NH
○	○	○	○	○

13
$$417$$
$$\underline{-\ 12}$$

439	429	425	405	NH
○	○	○	○	○

14 $9 + \square = 12$

2	3	4	5	NH
○	○	○	○	○

15
$$45$$
$$\underline{-\ 8}$$

_____

_____

_____

_____

16
$$515$$
$$\underline{+\ 46}$$

561	551	461	451	NH
○	○	○	○	○

17 $15 - 6 = \square$

7	8	10	11	NH
○	○	○	○	○

STOP

Directions: Darken the circle for the correct answer. If the correct answer is not given, darken the circle NH (Not Here). If there are no circles, write the answer on the lines.

1 Which number is between 72 and 95?

72		95

43	71	89	96
○	○	○	○

---

2 What number is in the ones place?

294

0	2	4	9
○	○	○	○

---

3 Which number names the greatest amount?

156	198	220	314
○	○	○	○

---

4 Which number is the same as six hundred ninety-two?

60,092	6,092	6,902	692
○	○	○	○

GO ON

71

5 Write the number that is one hundred more than five hundred thirty-eight.

538

---

6 Write the number that is missing in the pattern.

(65) (70) (75) (   ) (85)

---

7 What number makes the number sentence true?

23 + 17 = ☐ + 23

6   17   32   40

◯   ◯   ◯   ◯

---

8 Marta counts shirts. She begins with 13. Which shirt does Marta count as number 22?

13   14   15   ◯   ◯   ◯   ◯

GO ON ▶

9 Which fraction tells the part of the triangle that is shaded?

$\frac{1}{2}$	$\frac{1}{3}$	$\frac{1}{4}$	$\frac{2}{1}$
○	○	○	○

10 Which picture shows one-quarter of the buttons shaded?

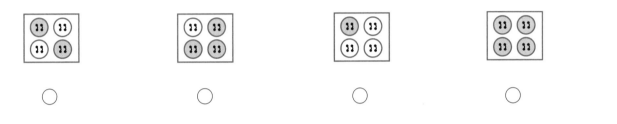

    ○   ○   ○   ○

11 Who is tallest?

Name	Height
Jimmy	45 in.
Ming	48 in.
Ralph	52 in.
Anna	60 in.

Jimmy	Ming	Ralph	Anna
○	○	○	○

12 Which shape comes next in the pattern?

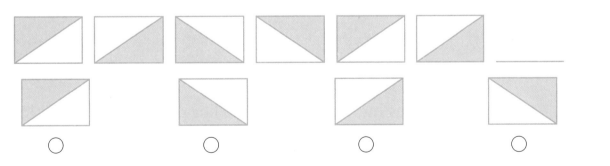

    ○   ○   ○   ○

GO ON ➡

Animals at Walker Park

1 paw = 1 animal

Deer   Raccoon   Fox   Rabbit

13 What animal does Walker Park have three of?

Deer   Raccoon   Fox   Rabbit
○   ○   ○   ○

14 How many foxes are there at Walker Park?

_____

_____

_____

_____

15 The clocks show the times Inga starts and ends her piano lesson. How long does her lesson last?

_____

_____

_____

_____

GO ON ▶

16 Which shape will NOT match exactly when folded on the dotted line?

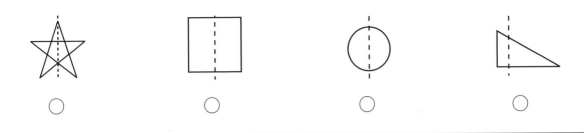

○   ○   ○   ○

17 Fred cut a shape from the card at the beginning of the row. Which shape did Fred cut out?

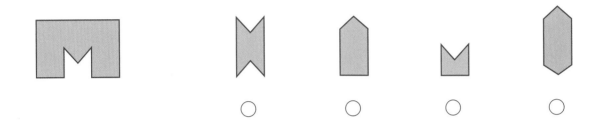

○   ○   ○   ○

18 Use an inch ruler. How long is this toy bus in inches?

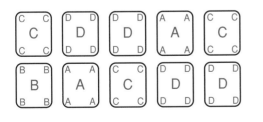

7   4   3   2

○   ○   ○   ○

19 Alice picks a card without looking. What letter is she most likely to pick?

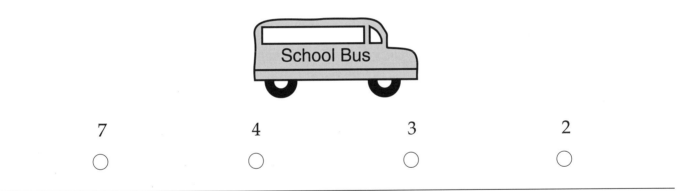

A   B   C   D

○   ○   ○   ○

GO ON

20 Which piece of chalk is the longest?

○   ○   ○   ○

21 What is the value of these coins?

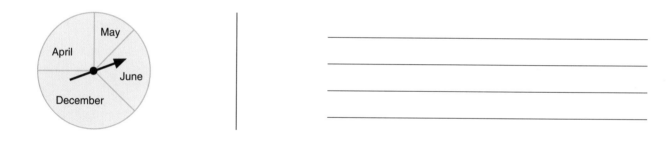

30¢   15¢   11¢   6¢

○   ○   ○   ○

22 Which month is this spinner least likely to land on?

_____

_____

_____

_____

23 What unit is best to use to measure the amount of juice in a jar?

Pounds   Teaspoons   Inches   Ounces

○   ○   ○   ○

GO ON ➡

24 Jenna is thinking of one of these numbers. Her number is inside the square and outside the circle. Her number is odd. What is Jenna's number?

11	13	12
16	14	15

16 ○   15 ○   13 ○   11 ○

---

25 Kyle is thinking of a number between 20 and 30. The sum of the digits is 8. Which is Kyle's number?

24 ○   26 ○   28 ○   29 ○

---

26 There are 16 children on a bus. Five more children get on the bus. Which number sentence shows how to find the total number of children on the bus?

○ $16 - 5 = \square$ ○ $16 + 5 = \square$

○ $16 - \square = 5$ ○ $5 + \square = 16$

LANGUAGE

========= PREWRITING, COMPOSING, AND EDITING =========

Directions: Darken the circle for the correct answer, or write the answer on the blank lines.

Sample A

Max is at summer camp. He will write a letter to his family telling about his favorite camp activities. Look at the three boxes below "Letter to My Family." Which idea will Max NOT write about in his letter?

Letter to My Family

The food at camp is good.	I like to sail in the morning.	We have fun swimming when it is hot.
○	○	○

THINK IT THROUGH You should have darkened the circle for the <u>first</u> choice. The answer is <u>The food at camp is good.</u> Adam wanted to write about activities in his letter. This is an idea.

STOP

Soccer Fun

Soccer is my favorite sport.
I like to run up and down the field.
Sometimes the ball I take away from the other team.
It is fun when I score a goal.

1 Read "Soccer Fun." Which of these sentences should be written next?

○ I play soccer after school.

○ My mother watches me play soccer.

○ Everyone cheers for me.

2 Look at the sentence in "Soccer Fun" that reads Sometimes the ball I take away from the other team. Is this sentence written correctly? Choose the way it should be written, or choose Correct the way it is.

○ The ball I take away sometimes from the other team.

○ Sometimes I take the ball away from the other team.

○ Correct the way it is.

3 Leila's teacher asked the students in the class to write a story about their favorite sport. Leila likes to play soccer. She decided to write about soccer. What should Leila do before she begins writing her story?

○ watch a soccer game

○ draw a picture of herself playing soccer

○ make a list of reasons she likes soccer

GO ON

4 Why will Leila write a story about soccer?

_____

_____

_____

_____

_____

_____

_____

TEST TIP

To answer question 4, you may need to reread the information about Leila in question 3.

GO ON ➡

Here is what Leila wrote in her story.

> The name of my team is the Panthers.
>
> We practice two times each week.
>
> To warm up, we <u>running</u> around the field.
> **(1)**
>
> We also <u>kick</u> the ball to each other.
> **(2)**
>
> My best friends are on my team.
>
> We have so much fun together.

5 Look at the underlined word with the number 2 under it. Did Leila use the right word? Choose the word that Leila should have used, or choose <u>Correct the way it is.</u>

kicking   kicked   Correct the way it is.

○   ○   ○

6 Look at the underlined word with the number 1 under it. Did Leila use the right word? Choose the word that Leila should have used, or choose <u>Correct the way it is.</u>

ran   run   Correct the way it is.

○   ○   ○

7 Dinah's family went on a trip. When Dinah got home, she made a book telling about the things she had seen and done on her trip. She is not sure how to spell the word <u>visit</u>. She will look it up in the dictionary. Which of these words will probably be on the same page as the word <u>visit</u>?

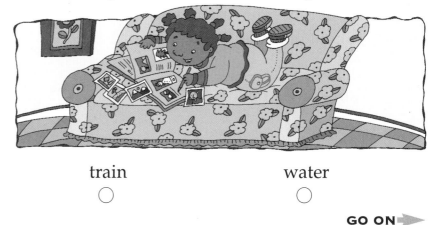

van   train   water

○   ○   ○

GO ON ➡

8 Look at the three boxes below "A Book About My Trip." Dinah is deciding what to write in her book. Which idea will Dinah NOT write about in her book?

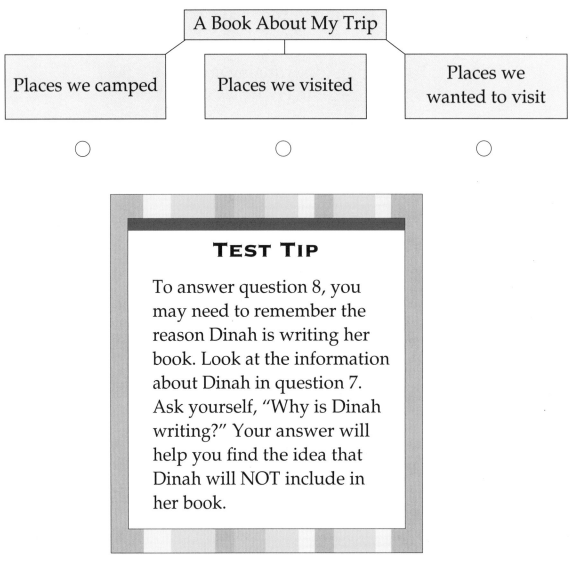

A Book About My Trip

Places we camped ○

Places we visited ○

Places we wanted to visit ○

TEST TIP

To answer question 8, you may need to remember the reason Dinah is writing her book. Look at the information about Dinah in question 7. Ask yourself, "Why is Dinah writing?" Your answer will help you find the idea that Dinah will NOT include in her book.

9 Dinah put this Table of Contents at the beginning of her book. What did Dinah write about on page 27?

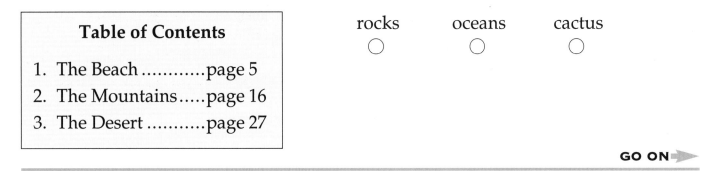

Table of Contents

1. The Beach ....page 5
2. The Mountains.....page 16
3. The Desert ....page 27

rocks ○   oceans ○   cactus ○

GO ON ▶

Here is one part of the story Dinah wrote.

We saw a very tall cactus in the desert.
We asked a park ranger about it.
The park ranger's name was <u>Mr. elkhorn</u>.
(1)
He said, "<u>A flower</u> will bloom on the cactus after it rains."
(2)

10 Look at the underlined words with the number 1 under them. Did Dinah capitalize these words correctly? Write your answer for the way Dinah should write the underlined words.

_____

_____

_____

_____

11 Look at the underlined words with the number 2 under them. Did Dinah capitalize these words correctly? Choose the words that show the correct capitalization, or choose <u>Correct the way it is</u>.

A Flower   a flower   Correct the way it is.
  ○   ○   ○

GO ON ▶

Here is one part of Dinah's finished story.

Travel Fun

My family went on a trip in June.
We slept in a tent every night.
My father cooked over a campfire.
We sang songs in school.
We went to many interesting places.

12 Which sentence does not belong in this story?

○ My family went on a trip in June.

○ My father cooked over a campfire.

○ We sang songs in school.

---

13 Dinah wants to tell about a beach she visited. Which of these sentences would she probably write?

○ We had a picnic in the park.

○ The huge waves crashed against the white sand.

○ I bought some colorful postcards.

TEST TIP

Remember that the ideas in a story or paragraph should all tell about the main idea. To answer question 12, find the sentence that does not tell about Dinah's trip with her family.

STOP

Directions: Darken the circle for the underlined word that is NOT spelled correctly.

| TRY THIS | Look at each of the underlined words carefully and say each of these words silently to yourself. Decide which words you know are spelled correctly. Then look at the other words to make your choice. |

Sample A

The <u>magical</u> king <u>granted</u> the shoemaker three <u>wishs</u>.
○ ○ ○

| THINK IT THROUGH | You should have darkened the circle for the last underlined word. <u>Wishs</u> is the word that is not spelled correctly. Wishes is spelled w-i-s-h-e-s. |

STOP

1   The car <u>started</u> <u>slideing</u> on the icy <u>highway</u>.
○ ○ ○

2   The <u>wave</u> <u>carryed</u> the shell onto the <u>beach</u>.
○ ○ ○

3   <u>Please</u> <u>sit</u> on the <u>char</u>.
○ ○ ○

4   Carley <u>loves</u> to <u>read</u> <u>storys</u> about pirates.
○ ○ ○

5   The <u>puppy</u> was sitting up and <u>beging</u> for a <u>treat</u>.
○ ○ ○

GO ON ➡

6 The horse tryed to eat my carrot.
    ○ ○   ○

7 My uncle was swiming in the ocean.
    ○   ○   ○

8 The garden is filled with menny pretty flowers.
    ○   ○   ○

9 We will go two the movies on Tuesday.
    ○   ○   ○

10 I heard the loud trane whistle.
    ○   ○ ○

11 The ice finally stopped driping.
    ○ ○ ○

12 The king and the queen walked togethir.
    ○   ○   ○

13 My best frend knows lots of funny riddles.
    ○ ○   ○

14 I would like to have a milion dollars.
    ○   ○ ○

STOP

Sample A

The school newspaper was looking for stories about people who worked in the town. Heather's father is a police officer. Heather decided to write a story about her father.

Look at the three boxes below "Writing a Story." What should Heather do before writing her story?

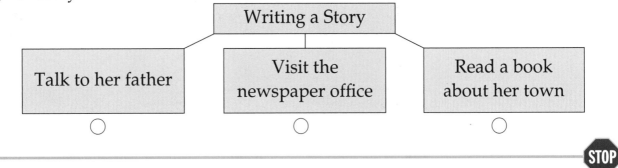

STOP

---

1 What should Heather do <u>before</u> she talks to her father?

○ Ride in a police car

○ Watch a movie about police officers

○ Make a list of questions to ask her father

GO ON

Here is the story Heather wrote.

A Police Officer's Job

My father is a police officer.
He has an important job.
My bike has a flat tire.
He helps people who are hurt.
Sometimes he directs cars.

2 Which of the sentences does NOT belong in Heather's story? Write the sentence that does NOT belong in this story.

_____

_____

_____

_____

Randy's teacher asked the students to write a story about something they would like to do when they get older. Randy likes to read stories about traveling in space. He also likes to study the stars and the planets through his telescope. He wants to take a trip to the moon when he is older. He wants to learn more about the moon before he writes his story. So he got a book from the library. This is the Table of Contents in the book Randy found at the library.

Table of Contents

3 When Randy looks at page 2, what will he read about?

○ the big holes on the moon

○ the miles between the earth and moon

○ the first person who visited the moon

GO ON ➡

4 Which page should Randy turn to if he wants to read about people who have visited the moon?

_____

_____

_____

_____

_____

_____

_____

_____

_____

TEST TIP

Remember that a Table of Contents helps you find information in a book. The chapter titles tell you what each chapter discusses. Read each chapter title carefully and think about what kind of information you would find in the chapter.

Here is one part of Randy's story.

> The big holes <u>is</u> called craters.
> **(1)**
> I would <u>like</u> to go inside a crater.
> **(2)**
> It would be like walking inside a cave.

5 Look at the word with the number 1 under it. Did Randy use the right word? Should he write <u>are</u>, <u>were</u>, or is the word correct the way it is? Write the word Randy should use.

_____

_____

6 Look at the word with the number 2 under it. Did Randy use the right word? Choose the correct word or choose <u>Correct the way it is</u>.

○ liking

○ likes

○ Correct the way it is.

GO ON →

Here is another part of Randy's story.

Seeing the Moon

The moon is very far away.
I would like to ride in a spaceship to get there.
A spacesuit I could wear to keep me safe.
I would like to see what is in the moon's big holes.

7 Which of these sentences would Randy probably write at the beginning of his story?

   ○ When I get older, I want to visit the moon.

   ○ The big holes are deep.

   ○ A spaceship moves very fast.

8 Look at the sentence that reads A spacesuit I could wear to keep me safe. Did Randy write this sentence correctly? Choose the correct sentence or choose Correct the way it is.

   ○ A spacesuit to keep me safe I could wear.

   ○ I could wear a spacesuit to keep me safe.

   ○ Correct the way it is.

GO ON ➡

Shakia is going to visit her Aunt Donna. Aunt Donna lives on a farm. Shakia decided to write a letter to let her aunt know when she would arrive. Here is the first part of Shakia's letter.

Dear Aunt Donna,

Thank you for inviting me to visit.
The farm this summer.
<u>May I stay for two weeks</u>
I want to learn how to take care of animals.

9 Which group of words in Shakia's letter does NOT make a complete sentence? Write the words here.

GO ON➤

10 Which sentence should Shakia write next in her letter?

    ◯ I want to milk and feed the cows and chickens.

    ◯ The cows I want to milk and the chickens I want to feed.

    ◯ I want to milk the cows and feed the chickens.

---

11 Look at the underlined sentence in Shakia's letter. Which punctuation mark should Shakia place at the end of the underlined sentence? Choose the word that ends with the correct punctuation.

    weeks?   weeks.   weeks!
     ◯   ◯   ◯

TEST TIP

To answer question 10, find the sentence that tells a clear idea. Notice that the first sentence is confusing. You cannot milk a chicken! Read the other two choices carefully. Choose the sentence that is complete and clear.

GO ON ➡

Here is the second part of Shakia's letter.

> I am leaving this <u>tuesday</u>.
> **(1)**
> <u>Will you pick me up at the bus station</u>
> **(2)**
> I can't wait to see you.
> Love,
> Shakia

12 Look at the underlined sentence with a number 2 under it. Which punctuation mark should Shakia place at the end of this sentence? Write the punctuation mark here.

_____

_____

_____

13 Look at the underlined word with the number 1 under it. Did Shakia capitalize this word correctly? Choose the correct way to capitalize this word, or choose <u>Correct the way it is.</u>

Tues Day ○   Tuesday ○   Correct the way it is. ○

TEST TIP

Remember some rules about capitalization. Always capitalize the first word in a sentence. Always capitalize the names of months and days of the week. Always capitalize people's names.

STOP

Directions: Darken the circle for the underlined word that is NOT spelled correctly.

14   Wher does your family like to swim?
     ○ ○   ○

15   Go down the hall and tern to the right.
      ○   ○   ○

16   The frog was hoping along the path.
      ○   ○   ○

17   Your dog is very frendly.
    ○ ○   ○

18   Watr the plants before you leave.
   ○   ○   ○

19   We saw many interesting butterflys in the woods.
          ○   ○   ○

20   Grandpa gave me three big pushs on the swing.
        ○   ○   ○

21   The boxs were stacked in the corner.
     ○   ○   ○

STOP

Directions: Darken the circle next to the best answer.

Sample A

Going to School

Jim lives on a farm. The farm is five miles from his school. He rides a bus to school because he lives too far to walk.

How does Jim get to school?

○ He walks.

○ His mom drives him in a car.

○ He rides a horse.

○ He rides a bus.

Curtis's Jobs

Mr. Ford asked Curtis to do some jobs. Curtis likes to help Mr. Ford. Mr. Ford always gives him a dollar for each job.

Curtis got a hose and soap. He washed the windows, the doors, and the trunk. Finally, Curtis washed the tires.

When Curtis was done, Mr. Ford looked at the car. "You worked very hard. I will give you two dollars," said Mr. Ford. "Tomorrow morning you will need a rake. I will pay you two more dollars if you do as well."

"Thank you, Mr. Ford. I will be back tomorrow," said Curtis.

1   Why did Mr. Ford give Curtis two dollars?

○ Curtis did a good job.

○ Curtis wanted to buy candy.

○ Curtis did two jobs.

○ Curtis needed a loan.

2   What did Curtis wash?

○ a bike

○ a car

○ a house

○ a dog

3   Curtis will go to Mr. Ford's—

○ in the middle of the night.

○ in the morning.

○ in the afternoon.

○ in the evening.

4   You can tell that tomorrow Curtis will—

○ trim trees.

○ mow the grass.

○ sweep the sidewalk.

○ rake leaves.

GO ON

Tia's Ride

Tia lived in the mountains with her family and a donkey named Clyde. Tia and Clyde went everywhere together. Clyde was a good mountain climber. He never slipped or fell. Tia was not as good at climbing. She had to be careful where she walked. When the path was dangerous, Tia would ride on Clyde's back. Tia rode the donkey on the path down to the stream. There were fish swimming in the stream. Tia and the donkey splashed in the cool, clear water. Later when they returned home, Tia gave Clyde a pail of food. Then Tia went inside for dinner.

5 **The boxes show things that happened in the story.**

Tia rode the donkey down to the stream.		Tia gave Clyde a pail of food.
1	2	3

What belongs in Box 2?

○ Tia went inside the house for dinner.

○ Clyde slipped on the path to the stream.

○ Tia and Clyde caught some fish.

○ Tia and Clyde splashed in the water.

6 **What is another good name for this story?**

○ "Walking in the Mountains"

○ "A Girl and Her Donkey"

○ "How to Train a Donkey"

○ "Fishing in Mountain Streams"

7 **Where did Tia and Clyde live?**

○ on a farm

○ in the mountains

○ in the city

○ by a store

8 **Why did Tia ride the donkey to the stream?**

○ The donkey was tired.

○ The path was long.

○ The path was dangerous.

○ The donkey hurt his foot.

 GO ON

Telling a Tree's Age

Have you ever looked closely at the top of a tree stump? You might see many rings. The rings are often narrow near the center of the tree and wider near the outside.

Each ring stands for a year of growth. As a tree grows, more and more rings are added. After the tree has been cut down, you can see the rings on the stump. The number of rings tells the tree's age. The more rings you count, the older the tree is.

9 **The rings on a tree stump are all—**

○ the same size.

○ narrow.

○ wide.

○ different sizes.

10 **How do you find the age of a tree?**

○ see if the rings are wide or narrow

○ count the leaves

○ count the rings

○ see how tall it is

11 **What can you say about a tree with many rings?**

○ It is old.

○ It is young.

○ It is tall.

○ It needs water.

12 **What is the best way to find out more about trees?**

○ Recycle paper.

○ Plant a garden.

○ Read a book about the life of a tree.

○ Read a list of things made from wood.

GO ON

Peanut Butter and Banana Bun

You will need:

1 hot dog bun

1 tablespoon peanut butter

1 banana

Follow these steps:

1. Spread the peanut butter on the bun.

2. Peel the banana and set it in the bun.

3. Slice the bun in half and serve one half per person.

If you like, you can add an optional topping. Sprinkle on coconut or pour on a little bit of honey. Or, think of your own special topping. "Peanut Butter and Banana Bun" is great with or without toppings.

13 **Right after you spread the peanut butter, you should—**

○ slice the bun in half.

○ serve the bun.

○ spread butter.

○ add the banana.

14 **"Peanut Butter and Banana Bun" is most like a—**

○ soup.

○ sandwich.

○ salad.

○ cookie.

15 **How many servings will each banana and bun make?**

○ four

○ three

○ two

○ one

16 **In these directions, optional means—**

○ something you may or may not do.

○ something you must do.

○ something you cook.

○ something you taste.

GO ON➔

Maciel Visits the Lighthouse

Maciel and her mother went to the beach in Cape May, New Jersey, last summer. One day they went to see the lighthouse.

Maciel and her mom climbed to the top of the tower. From there they could see very far. They saw miles of ocean and beach. It was a beautiful sight.

Mr. Foreman, the man who works at the lighthouse, told Maciel and her mom all about it. The Cape May Lighthouse is over 130 years old. It is all white, and it is 165 feet tall. It has a very strong light. Mr. Foreman said that the lighthouse is still very important to sailors. Sailors can see its light from 24 miles out at sea. The light helps ships come into Delaware Bay.

Mr. Foreman told Maciel and her mom how the sailors take care of the lighthouse. Their <u>tasks</u> are cleaning the light and making sure it is working. Mr. Foreman said that many people who live in Cape May also help keep the lighthouse in good shape. They want others to enjoy it for many years to come. Some people help fix parts of the lighthouse. Some clean the lighthouse. Others paint it.

Maciel can't wait to visit the lighthouse again next summer. She wants Mr. Foreman to show the lighthouse to her best friend, Josephine.

GO ON ➡

17 In this story, Mr. Foreman is—

○ a sailor who cleans the light at the lighthouse.

○ the man who works at the lighthouse.

○ Maciel's father.

○ Maciel's best friend.

18 Why is it important to take care of the lighthouse?

○ so that Mr. Foreman can have a job

○ so people can look out of the tower

○ so that sailors at sea can find land

○ so that visitors have a place to go

19 How does Maciel feel at the end of the story?

○ She is tired and wants to leave.

○ She wants to live in the lighthouse.

○ She worries that sailors do not take care of the lighthouse.

○ She is excited about the visit and wants to come back.

20 What does the word <u>tasks</u> in this story mean?

○ jobs

○ friends

○ joys

○ games

21 This story was written mainly to—

○ tell about big ships.

○ ask for help in fixing the lighthouse.

○ tell about a special lighthouse.

○ tell how to build a lighthouse.

22 Which of these is another good name for this story?

○ "Maciel and Her Mom Have Fun at the Beach"

○ "A Visit to a Lighthouse"

○ "Sailing in Delaware Bay"

○ "How to Take Care of a Lighthouse"

GO ON➡

All About Ducks

Ducks are interesting birds. They can fly in the air, and they can walk on the land. Mostly, they like to swim in the water. Ponds and streams are full of good things to eat. There are little fish, big bugs, and tender plants. Ducks can swim very fast. They have big feet for pushing the water. They cannot walk as fast as they swim. On land, ducks must be careful. A fox or a wolf might catch them.

23 **What is another good name for this story?**

- ○ "Why Ducks Like Water"
- ○ "Why Ducks Fly"
- ○ "What Ducks Like to Eat"
- ○ "How to Catch a Duck"

24 **How do big feet help ducks?**

- ○ Big feet help them walk fast.
- ○ Big feet help them catch bugs.
- ○ Big feet help them push the water.
- ○ Big feet help them hide from foxes.

25 **What is something that ducks do not do?**

- ○ swim
- ○ climb
- ○ walk
- ○ fly

26 **Why might a fox want to catch a duck?**

- ○ to eat it
- ○ to play with it
- ○ to see who is faster
- ○ to learn to swim

STOP

PRACTICE TEST 2

READING VOCABULARY

Directions: Darken the circle under the compound word.

1   sorry ○   circus ○   ladybug ○

2   open ○   inside ○   under ○

3   before ○   something ○   story ○

4   balloon ○   myself ○   making ○

5   quiet ○   again ○   cupcake ○

6   penny ○   wishing ○   suitcase ○

Directions: Darken the circle under the word that shows the correct plural noun.

7   more than one tent
    tens ○   tents ○   tentes ○

8   more than one farmer
    farmeres ○   farmer ○   farmers ○

9   more than one box
    boxes ○   boxs ○   boxies ○

10 more than one cherry
    cherries ○   cherrys ○   cherryes ○

11 more than one leaf
    leafes ○   leafs ○   leaves ○

12 more than one animal
    animales ○   animals ○   animalls ○

STOP

Directions: Darken the circle under the word that has the same sound or sounds as the underlined part of the first word in each row.

13 n<u>ea</u>r

   rocky   speed   knee
    ◯   ◯   ◯

14 t<u>i</u>me

   shy   lip   feel
    ◯   ◯   ◯

15 str<u>o</u>ng

   toe   mouth   jaw
    ◯   ◯   ◯

16 b<u>ow</u>

   front   road   should
    ◯   ◯   ◯

17 v<u>oi</u>ce

   lost   enjoy   who
    ◯   ◯   ◯

18 h<u>o</u>pped

   locking   only   worn
    ◯   ◯   ◯

Directions: Darken the circle under the word that rhymes with the first word in each row.

19 rain

   plate   play   plane
    ◯   ◯   ◯

20 speed

   feet   knee   bead
    ◯   ◯   ◯

21 eight

   gate   day   note
    ◯   ◯   ◯

22 hope

   no   soap   hop
    ◯   ◯   ◯

23 chair

   chore   cheer   pear
    ◯   ◯   ◯

24 night

   kite   kit   cat
    ◯   ◯   ◯

STOP

Directions: Darken the circle next to the answer that best completes the sentence.

25 Closer means—
- ○ nearer
- ○ around
- ○ away
- ○ farther

26 To whisper is to—
- ○ talk softly
- ○ play a game
- ○ run a race
- ○ sing loudly

27 To hunt means to—
- ○ talk
- ○ sit on
- ○ break
- ○ look for

28 If something is still, it is not—
- ○ sorry
- ○ strong
- ○ moving
- ○ sleeping

29 A carpet is most like a—
- ○ chair
- ○ window
- ○ rug
- ○ truck

30 Foolish means—
- ○ next
- ○ silly
- ○ last
- ○ sleepy

31 A subway is a kind of—
- ○ train
- ○ walk
- ○ book
- ○ number

32 A chuckle is a kind of—
- ○ song
- ○ laugh
- ○ story
- ○ river

33 A dish is most like a—
- ○ desk
- ○ plate
- ○ pillow
- ○ cup

GO ON ➡

Directions: Darken the circle next to the answer that best answers the question or fill in the answer on the lines.

34

Is it my turn to <u>bat</u>?

In which sentence does <u>bat</u> mean the same as it does above?

○ A <u>bat</u> is an interesting animal.

○ Please hand me the other <u>bat</u>.

○ Let's <u>bat</u> some ideas around.

○ I will <u>bat</u> the ball to the fence.

35

Can you <u>float</u> on your back in the water?

In which sentence does <u>float</u> mean the same as it does above?

○ Dad made me a root beer <u>float</u>.

○ Which <u>float</u> did you like?

○ The small boat began to <u>float</u> on the lake.

○ Carol had a <u>float</u> to play with in the pool.

36

We watched the sun <u>dip</u> below the trees.

Write a sentence in which <u>dip</u> means the same as it does above.

_____

_____

_____

_____

_____

_____

_____

37

We climbed over the steep <u>bank</u> to the lake.

In which sentence does <u>bank</u> mean the same as it does above?

○ My <u>bank</u> is in a big, gray building.

○ She has a new purple piggy <u>bank</u>.

○ Don't <u>bank</u> on his promise.

○ Flowers grow along the river <u>bank</u>.

GO ON➡

Directions: Darken the circle next to the answer that best completes the sentence or fill in the answer on the lines.

38 That painting is <u>famous</u> all over the world. <u>Famous</u> means—

○ well-known

○ cheap

○ new

○ funny

39 The bridge is closely <u>modeled</u> after one in England. <u>Modeled</u> means—

○ paid

○ painted

○ added

○ copied

40 I tried but I couldn't <u>budge</u> the heavy box. <u>Budge</u> means—

○ buy

○ pack

○ move

○ seal

41 It is dangerous to play with matches because they could <u>harm</u> someone. <u>Harm</u> means—

○ look

○ hurt

○ help

○ hear

42 He will <u>compose</u> a new song for the movie. What does <u>compose</u> mean?

_____

_____

_____

_____

43 Her truck has <u>tough</u> tires that last a long time. <u>Tough</u> means—

○ little

○ strong

○ many

○ old

44 We tried to be quiet and <u>conceal</u> the surprise. <u>Conceal</u> means—

○ hide

○ miss

○ show

○ end

STOP

PART 1: MATH PROBLEM SOLVING

Directions: Darken the circle for the correct answer, or write the answer on the lines.

1 Which brush is the fifth brush from the bucket?

2 Which number means two hundreds, three tens, and four ones?

234	2,034	20,304	200,304
○	○	○	○

3 Which number is between 43 and 68?

43		68

39	41	55	71
○	○	○	○

4 Which number is the same as one hundred seventy-three?

173	1,730	1,073	10,073
○	○	○	○

GO ON➡

5 How many marbles are there in this picture?

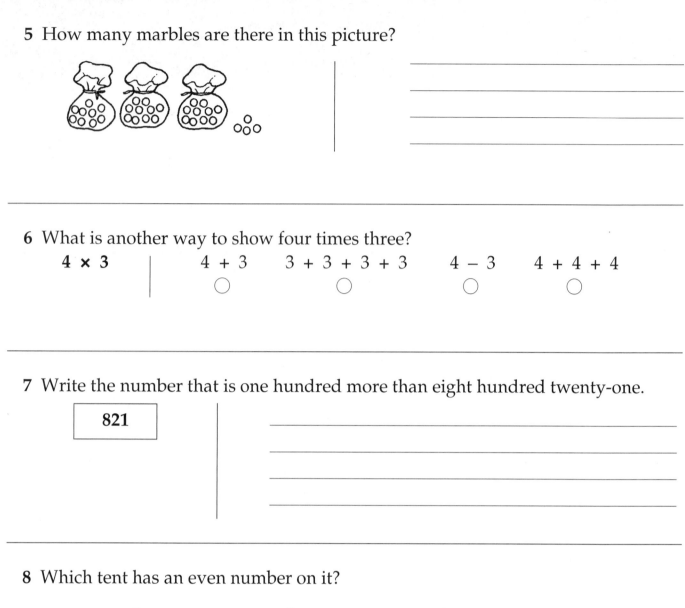

_____
_____
_____
_____

6 What is another way to show four times three?

4 × 3 | 4 + 3   3 + 3 + 3 + 3   4 − 3   4 + 4 + 4
        ○   ○   ○   ○

7 Write the number that is one hundred more than eight hundred twenty-one.

| 821 |

_____
_____
_____
_____

8 Which tent has an even number on it?

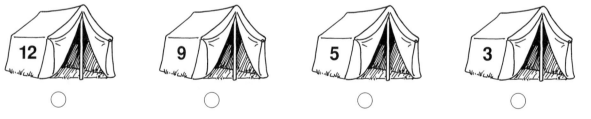

12   9   5   3
○   ○   ○   ○

GO ON ➡

9 What number makes this number sentence true?

4 + ☐ = 4

    0 ○   1 ○   4 ○   8 ○

---

10 Which number sentence can describe this picture?

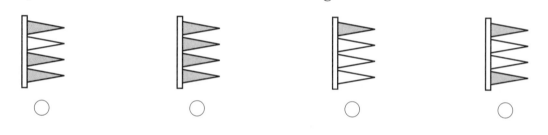

○ 10 + 9 = 19   ○ 10 − 8 = 2

○ 9 − 1 = 8   ○ 9 + 1 = 10

---

11 Which picture shows three-fourths of the flags shaded?

○   ○   ○   ○

---

12 What number is missing in this pattern?

36	33		27	24

  25 ○   30 ○   34 ○   35 ○

GO ON ➡

13 Which shape is NOT divided into fourths?

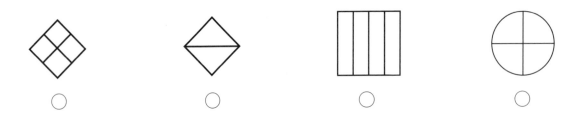

○   ○   ○   ○

---

14 Felipe is counting stamps. He begins at 73. Which stamp will Felipe count as number 83?

73   74   75   ○   ○ ○   ○

---

15 Which fraction tells what part of the circle is shaded?

$\frac{1}{4}$	$\frac{1}{5}$	$\frac{4}{5}$	$\frac{4}{1}$
○	○	○	○

GO ON ➡

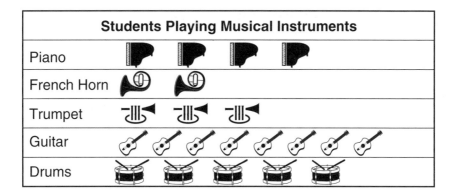

Each instrument = 1 student

16 How many students play guitar?

4   5   8   9
○   ○   ○   ○

17 How many more students play drums than trumpets?

_____

_____

_____

_____

18 Carly folded a card and cut out a shape. Which shape did Carly cut out?

○   ○   ○   ○

GO ON➡

19 Which player scored the fewest number of points?

Lou	Laurie	Alex	Patti
卌 卌	卌	I	III

_____
_____
_____
_____

20 Which pencil is the shortest?

○   ○   ○   ○

21 Which shape is exactly the same as the shape at the left?

○   ○   ○   ○

22 Tina puts these shapes in a box. She picks one without looking. Which shape is she most likely to pick?

○   ○   ○   ○

GO ON➡

23 What time is shown on this clock?

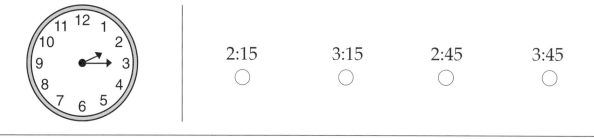

2:15 ○   3:15 ○   2:45 ○   3:45 ○

24 Which shape will not match exactly when it is folded on the dotted line?

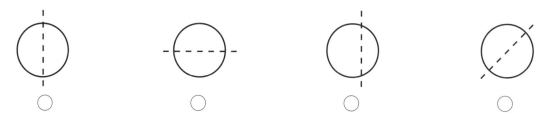

○   ○   ○   ○

25 Use a centimeter ruler. How long is the pen in centimeters?

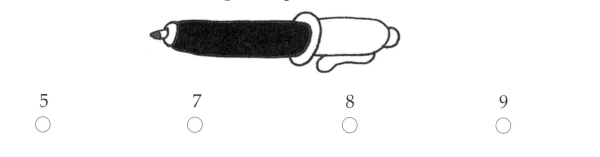

5 ○   7 ○   8 ○   9 ○

26 What is the value of these coins?

6¢ ○   11¢ ○   26¢ ○   30¢ ○

STOP

Sample A

$$102 - 12 = \square$$

78	80	82	90	NH
Ⓐ	Ⓑ	Ⓒ	Ⓓ	Ⓔ

STOP

For questions 1–17, darken the circle for the correct answer. If the correct answer is not here, darken the circle for NH. If no choices are given, write the answer.

1

$$\begin{array}{r} 53 \\ 4 \\ + \ 21 \\ \hline \end{array}$$

77	78	87	88	NH
Ⓐ	Ⓑ	Ⓒ	Ⓓ	Ⓔ

2

$$\begin{array}{r} 400 \\ - \ 50 \\ \hline \end{array}$$

150	300	350	450	NH
Ⓕ	Ⓖ	Ⓗ	Ⓙ	Ⓚ

3

$$8 + \square = 16$$

5	7	9	11	NH
Ⓐ	Ⓑ	Ⓒ	Ⓓ	Ⓔ

4

$$\begin{array}{r} 28 \\ + \ 87 \\ \hline \end{array}$$

105	115	151	155	NH
Ⓕ	Ⓖ	Ⓗ	Ⓙ	Ⓚ

5

$$\begin{array}{r} 54 \\ - \ 8 \\ \hline \end{array}$$

42	44	46	48	NH
Ⓐ	Ⓑ	Ⓒ	Ⓓ	Ⓔ

6

$$\begin{array}{r} 307 \\ - \ 125 \\ \hline \end{array}$$

182	187	282	432	NH
Ⓕ	Ⓖ	Ⓗ	Ⓙ	Ⓚ

7

$$\begin{array}{r} 99 \\ + \ 98 \\ \hline \end{array}$$

8

$$\begin{array}{r} 71 \\ - \ 9 \\ \hline \end{array}$$

GO ON

9

$$528$$
$$+\ 82$$

446   600   610   688   NH
Ⓐ   Ⓑ   Ⓒ   Ⓓ   Ⓔ

10

$$777 - 333 = \square$$

4   44   444   555   NH
Ⓕ   Ⓖ   Ⓗ   Ⓙ   Ⓚ

11

$$911$$
$$-\ 903$$

7   14   80   108   NH
Ⓐ   Ⓑ   Ⓒ   Ⓓ   Ⓔ

12

$$456$$
$$-\ 321$$

135   153   333   777   NH
Ⓕ   Ⓖ   Ⓗ   Ⓙ   Ⓚ

13

$$45 + 4 + 12 = \square$$

49   57   61   97   NH
Ⓐ   Ⓑ   Ⓒ   Ⓓ   Ⓔ

14

$$82 - \square = 75$$

_____

_____

_____

_____

---

15 There were 34 students on a school bus. At the first stop, 5 students got off the bus. How many students were still on the bus?

25   29   30   39   NH
Ⓕ   Ⓖ   Ⓗ   Ⓙ   Ⓚ

---

16 Pam and Rosa ran a race. Pam ran the race in 58 seconds. Rosa ran the race in 47 seconds. How many seconds faster was Rosa?

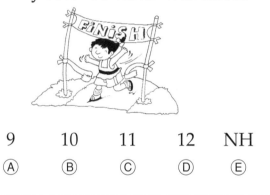

9   10   11   12   NH
Ⓐ   Ⓑ   Ⓒ   Ⓓ   Ⓔ

---

17 Bonnie works on a big puzzle. She has put 119 pieces together. There are 131 more pieces to put together. How many pieces are there in all?

200   250   300   350   NH
Ⓕ   Ⓖ   Ⓗ   Ⓙ   Ⓚ

STOP

LANGUAGE

1 Ingrid was having a birthday party. She was going to write her own party invitations. This is what she first wrote.

> I <u>hope</u> to see you at my party.
> Please let me know if you can come.
>   Your friend,
>   Ingrid

Look at the underlined word. Did Ingrid use the correct word? Choose the correct word or choose <u>Correct the way it is.</u>

hoped   hoping   Correct the way it is.
○   ○   ○

2 Ingrid realized that she had to let everyone know when her party was. Here is what Ingrid added to her invitation.

> I am having a birthday party at my house.
> On Friday at two o'clock.
> We will play games.

Which group of words is NOT a complete sentence?

○ I am having a birthday party.
○ On Friday at two o'clock.
○ We will play games.

GO ON ➡

3

Look at the three boxes below the box that reads <u>Writing Invitations</u>. What did Ingrid NOT write about in her invitations?

Sal's class was studying food and nutrition. The teacher asked the students to keep a diary for one week telling what kinds of foods they ate. She wanted them to find out if they ate healthy meals and snacks. Here is the first part of Sal's diary.

<u>A Big Breakfast</u>

I was hungry when I woke up.

I poured a glass of milk for everyone.

A glass of orange juice I also drank.

Father made banana muffins.

4 Which sentence will Sal probably write next?

○ I didn't drink all of my milk.

○ I will eat an apple for a snack.

○ The muffins were so good that I ate two.

GO ON➡

5 Look at the sentence that reads <u>A glass of orange juice I also drank</u>. Did Sal write this sentence correctly? Choose the correct sentence, or choose <u>Correct the way it is</u>.

○ I also drank a glass of orange juice.

○ I drank a glass also of orange juice.

○ Correct the way it is.

6 What did Sal do <u>before</u> he wrote in his diary?

○ ask his mother what his family will eat for dinner

○ make a list of healthy foods

○ think about the food he ate during the day

7 Why did Sal write a diary?

○ to find out if he eats good food

○ to write a food menu

○ to tell about his favorite foods

GO ON

I <u>gone</u> to a friend's house for dinner.
  (1)

We ate hot dogs.

Hot dogs <u>are</u> my favorite food.
      (2)

We had salad and peas, too.

Of course, I drank another glass of milk.

8 Look at the word with the number 2 under it. Did Sal use the correct word?
Choose the correct word, or choose <u>Correct the way it is.</u>

is   was   Correct the way it is.
○   ○   ○

9 Look at the word with the number 1 under it. Did Sal use the correct word?
Choose the correct word, or choose <u>Correct the way it is.</u>

is going   went   Correct the way it is.
○   ○   ○

GO ON

Ellen's class is learning about how people lived about 50 years ago. Her teacher asked the students to talk to a grandparent or older neighbor to get more information. Then the students are to write a story telling what they learned. Ellen talked to her grandmother.

10 Ellen is not sure how to spell the word <u>television</u>. She will look it up in the dictionary. Which word will probably be on the same page as <u>television</u>?

hay	chicken	train
○	○	○

11 Look at the three boxes under the box that says "In Grandma's Time." What will Ellen NOT write about in her story?

How people traveled	Games people played	Where Grandma lives
○	○	○

GO ON➡

Ellen put this Table of Contents at the front of her story.

Table of Contents

12 What did Ellen write about on page 3?

    long skirts   milking cows   riding horses

      ○   ○   ○

Here is the first part of Ellen's story.

When Grandma Was Young

Grandma lived on a farm when she was little.

The family grew most of their own food.

They grew corn, beans, and potatoes.

Grandma shops at the store on Friday.

They had to raise cows and chickens for meat.

13 Ellen wants to tell how Grandma's family cooked food. Which sentence would she probably write next?

○ Grandma cooked food in a big black pan on a wood stove.

○ The stove made the kitchen hot in the summer.

○ Grandma helped make bread every day.

GO ON➡

14 Which of these sentences does NOT belong in Ellen's story?

○ Grandma lived on a farm when she was little.

○ They grew corn, beans, and potatoes.

○ Grandma shops at the store on Friday.

The family could not grow everything they needed.

They had to buy things like flour and sugar.

"<u>Are you ready</u> for some fun?" Great Grandpa would ask.
(1)

Then the family knew it was time to go to town.

They would visit <u>mr barton's</u> store.
(2)

---

15 Look at the underlined words with the number 2 under them. Did Ellen capitalize these words correctly? Choose the correct words, or choose <u>Correct the way it is.</u>

     mr. Barton's   Mr. Barton's   Correct the way it is.

         ○   ○   ○

---

16 Look at the underlined words with the number 1 under them. Did Ellen capitalize these words correctly? Choose the correct words, or choose <u>Correct the way it is.</u>

     are you ready   Are you Ready   Correct the way it is.

         ○   ○   ○

GO ON➡

Kareem likes to go fishing. Every Saturday he walks to a stream near his house. One Saturday he caught a type of fish he had never seen before. Kareem went to the library to check out a book about fish. He wanted to find out what kind of fish he had caught.

17 In which part of the book should Kareem look to find out about the topics the book will discuss?

Table of contents   Title page   First chapter
    ◯   ◯   ◯

Kareem decided to write a story about the fish he caught. Here is the first part of Kareem's story.

> <u>A Rainbow Fish</u>
> I went fishing.
> On Saturday morning.
> I caught a fish I have never seen before.

18 Kareem wanted to describe the fish he caught. Which sentence should he write?

◯ Pink and blue stripes the fish had on its body.

◯ On its body pink and blue stripes the fish had.

◯ The fish had pink and blue stripes on its body.

GO ON ➡

19 Which group of words does NOT make a complete sentence?

- ○ I went fishing.

- ○ On Saturday morning.

- ○ I caught a fish I have never seen before.

Here is the second part of Kareem's story.

I did not know what kind of fish it was.

I went to the library to look in a book.

"Where are the books about fish" I asked.
   (1)

The librarian helped me.

I found a picture of the fish.
   (2)

It was called a rainbow trout.

---

20 Look at the underlined word with the number 2 under it. Did Kareem use the correct word? Choose the correct word, or choose <u>Correct the way it is</u>.

finding   finds   Correct the way it is.

○   ○   ○

GO ON➡

21 Look at the underlined words with the number 1 under them. Which punctuation mark should Kareem place at the end of this sentence? Write the punctuation mark here.

_____

GO ON➡

Directions: Darken the circle under the word that does NOT have the correct spelling.

22 Dad <u>bought</u> two new <u>leashs</u> for our <u>dog</u>.
     ○   ○   ○

23 Grover is <u>diging</u> a <u>hole</u> to bury his dog <u>bone</u>.
     ○   ○   ○

24 Angie is <u>bakeing</u> a <u>birthday</u> <u>cake</u>.
     ○   ○   ○

25 John <u>walkt</u> to the <u>store</u> to <u>buy</u> milk.
     ○   ○   ○

26 The <u>baby</u> <u>cryed</u> herself to <u>sleep</u>.
     ○   ○   ○

27 Water is <u>driping</u> off the <u>roof</u> of the <u>house</u>.
     ○   ○   ○

28 Do you <u>like</u> to eat <u>cherrys</u> for a <u>snack</u>?
     ○   ○   ○

29 We are <u>moveing</u> to <u>another</u> <u>state</u>.
     ○   ○   ○

STOP

Letter answers are provided for each question. When the first choice is correct, the answer is A. When the second choice is correct, the answer is B. When the third or fourth choices are correct, the answers are C or D.

Unit 1:
Six Reading Skills
pp. 8–9   1. A 2. C 3. D 4. A 5. A 6. B
pp. 10–11   1. C 2. A 3. D 4. C 5. A 6. A
pp. 12–13   1. D 2. B 3. D 4. C 5. C 6. C
pp. 14–15   1. A 2. D 3. C 4. C 5. A 6. D
pp. 16–17   1. B 2. C 3. D
pp. 18–19   1. C 2. A 3. B 4. C 5. C
pp. 20–21   1. B 2. D 3. C 4. C 5. A 6. B
pp. 22–23   1. A 2. B 3. B 4. D 5. A
pp. 24–25   1. D 2. A 3. A 4. C 5. B
pp. 26–27   1. C 2. A 3. D 4. A 5. C 6. A 7. D
pp. 28–29   1. A 2. C 3. B 4. C 5. A 6. B
pp. 30–31   1. A 2. B 3. B 4. C
pp. 32–33   1. B 2. A 3. B 4. B 5. C

Unit 2:
Reading Comprehension
pp. 34–39   SA. C 1. B 2. because it was about to rain 3. D 4. C 5. The mouse woke him up. 6. C 7. A 8. He misses Harry. 9. D 10. D 11. A 12. B 13. C 14. A 15. C 16. Students volunteer to help others and earn a volunteer pin. 17. A 18. B 19. C 20. D 21. A 22. For example: Dawn's Special Part
pp. 40–43   SA. A 1. D 2. A 3. B 4. in the sun 5. C 6. C 7. A 8. They have big eyes. 9. D 10. D 11. For example: tell someone at camp about his adventure 12. B 13. B 14. C 15. C 16. B 17. C

Unit 3:
Reading Vocabulary
p. 44   SA. A 1. D 2. B 3. C 4. C 5. A 6. B
p. 45   SA. A 1. B 2. I heard the telephone ring.
p. 46   SA. C 1. not allowed 2. A 3. A 4. C
p. 47   SA. C 1. A 2. B 3. A 4. C 5. A 6. B 7. C 8. B
p. 48   SA. B 1. C 2. B 3. C 4. A 5. B 6. C 7. A 8. C
p. 49   SA. A 1. A 2. C 3. C 4. B 5. C 6. B 7. B 8. B
p. 50   SA. C 1. C 2. A 3. A 4. B 5. C 6. B 7. C 8. B
pp. 51–54   1. D 2. A 3. C 4. A 5. D 6. B 7. D 8. I visited my aunt last week. 9. A 10. B 11. B 12. B 13. C 14. A 15. B 16. B 17. C 18. B 19. A 20. C 21. B 22. B 23. A 24. C 25. C 26. B 27. C 28. C 29. B 30. A 31. C 32. C 33. B 34. A 35. C 36. B

Unit 4:
Math Problem-Solving Plan
p. 56   **Step 1.** How much did Paul pay for three apples? **Step 2.** First apple is 25¢, additional apples are 20¢ each. **Step 3.** Add. **Step 4.** 25¢ + 20¢ + 20¢ = 65¢ **Step 5.** Yes, because when you add the costs of the apples the total is 65¢.
p. 57   **Step 1.** To find Jenny's number. **Step 2.** The number is less than 9 and greater than 5. It is odd. **Step 3.** Use logical thinking. **Step 4.** Only 6, 7, and 8 are greater than 5 and less than 9. Of these, only 7 is odd, so it is Jenny's number. **Step 5.** Yes, because 7 is the only possible answer.

Unit 5:
Math Problem Solving
p. 58   SA. C 1. 9 2. D 3. B

p. 59   SA. C 1. A 2. A 3. 0 4. B

p. 60   SA. C 1. C 2. 25 3. B

p. 61   SA. C 1. 3 2. D

p. 62   SA. C 1. D 2. B 3. B

p. 63   SA. D 1. 6 2. B 3. A

p. 64   SA. B 1. C 2. C 3. 32 4. A

pp. 65–67   SA. C 1. B 2. A 3. B 4. 25
5. C 6. B 7. E 8. A 9. C 10. D 11. C
12. D 13. 197 14. C

p. 68   SA. B 1. B 2. D 3. B 4. C 5. E
6. 34

pp. 69–70   1. B 2. 35 3. C 4. C 5. A
6. E 7. C 8. D 9. B 10. D 11. C 12. A
13. D 14. B 15. 37 16. A 17. E

pp. 71–77   1. C 2. C 3. D 4. D 5. 638
6. 80 7. B 8. B 9. A 10. C 11. D 12. B
13. B 14. 7 15. 30 minutes 16. D 17. C
18. D 19. D 20. A 21. B 22. May
23. D 24. D 25. B 26. C

Unit 6:
Language
pp. 78–84   SA. A 1. C 2. B 3. C 4. to
tell why she likes soccer 5. C 6. B
7. A 8. C 9. C 10. Mr. Elkhorn 11. C
12. C 13. B

pp. 85–86   SA. C 1. B 2. B 3. C 4. C
5. B 6. B 7. B 8. B 9. A 10. B 11. C
12. C 13. A 14. B

pp. 87–94   SA. A 1. C 2. My bike has a
flat tire. 3. B 4. 25 5. are 6. C 7. A
8. B 9. The farm this summer. 10. C
11. A 12. ? 13. B 14. A 15. B 16. B
17. C 18. A 19. B 20. B 21. A

Unit 7:
Practice Test 1:
Reading Comprehension
pp. 95–101   SA. D 1. A 2. B 3. B 4. D
5. D 6. B 7. B 8. C 9. D 10. C 11. A

12. C 13. D 14. B 15. C 16. A 17. B
18. C 19. D 20. A 21. C 22. B 23. A
24. C 25. B 26. A

Unit 8:
Practice Test 2:
Reading Vocabulary
pp. 102–106   SA. C 1. C 2. B 3. B 4. B
5. C 6. C 7. B 8. C 9. A 10. A 11. C
12. B 13. C 14. A 15. C 16. B 17. B
18. A 19. C 20. C 21. A 22. B 23. C
24. A 25. A 26. A 27. D 28. C 29. C
30. B 31. A 32. B 33. B 34. D 35. C
36. For example: Did you dip your
cookie into your milk? 37. D 38. A
39. D 40. C 41. B 42. write 43. B
44. A

Unit 9:
Practice Test 3:
Part 1: Math Problem Solving
pp. 107–113   1. B 2. A 3. C 4. A 5. 33
6. B 7. 921 8. A 9. A 10. D 11. A 12. B
13. B 14. A 15. B 16. C 17. 2 18. C
19. Alex 20. B 21. C 22. A 23. A
24. C 25. B 26. C

Part 2: Math Procedures
pp. 114–115   SA. D 1. B 2. H 3. E 4. G
5. C 6. F 7. 197 8. 62 9. C 10. H 11. E
12. F 13. C 14. 7 15. G 16. C 17. G

Unit 10:
Practice Test 4:
Language
pp. 116–126   1. C 2. B 3. A 4. C 5. A
6. C 7. A 8. C 9. B 10. C 11. C 12. B
13. A 14. C 15. B 16. C 17. A 18. C
19. B 20. C 21. fish? 22. B 23. A 24. A
25. A 26. B 27. A 28. B 29. A